Quod scriptura, non iubet vetat

The Latin translates, "What is not commanded in scripture, is forbidden:'

On the Cover: Baptists rejoice to hold in common with other evangelicals the main principles of the orthodox Christian faith. However, there are points of difference and these differences are significant. In fact, because these differences arise out of God's revealed will, they are of vital importance. Hence, the barriers of separation between Baptists and others can hardly be considered a trifling matter. To suppose that Baptists are kept apart solely by their views on Baptism or the Lord's Supper is a regrettable misunderstanding. Baptists hold views which distinguish them from Catholics, Congregationalists, Episcopalians, Lutherans, Methodists, Pentecostals, and Presbyterians, and the differences are so great as not only to justify, but to demand, the separate denominational existence of Baptists. Some people think Baptists ought not teach and emphasize their differences but as E.J. Forrester stated in 1893, "Any denomination that has views which justify its separate existence, is bound to promulgate those views. If those views are of sufficient importance to justify a separate existence, they are important enough to create a duty for their promulgation ... the very same reasons which justify the separate existence of any denomination make it the duty of that denomination to teach the distinctive doctrines upon which its separate existence rests." If Baptists have a right to a separate denominational life, it is their duty to propagate their distinctive principles, without which their separate life cannot be justified or maintained.

Many among today's professing Baptists have an agenda to revise the Baptist distinctives and redefine what it means to be a Baptist. Others don't understand why it even matters. The books being reproduced in the *Baptist Distinctives Series* are republished in order that Baptists from the past may state, explain and defend the primary Baptist distinctives as they understood them. It is hoped that this Series will provide a more thorough historical perspective on what it means to be distinctively Baptist.

The Lord Jesus Christ asked, *"And why call ye me, Lord, Lord, and do not the things which I say?"* (Luke 6:46). The immediate context surrounding this question explains what it means to be a true disciple of Christ. Addressing the same issue, Christ's question is meant to show that a confession of discipleship to the Lord Jesus Christ is inconsistent and untrue if it is not accompanied with a corresponding submission to His authoritative commands. Christ's question teaches us that a true recognition of His authority as Lord inevitably includes a submission to the authority of His Word. Hence, with this question Christ has made it forever impossible to separate His authority as King from the authority of His Word. These two principles—the authority of Christ as King and the authority of His Word—are the two most fundamental Baptist distinctives. The first gives rise to the second and out of these two all the other Baptist distinctives emanate. As F.M. Iams wrote in 1894, "Loyalty to Christ as King, manifesting itself in a constant and unswerving obedience to His will as revealed in His written Word, is the real source of all the Baptist distinctives:' In the search for the *primary* Baptist distinctive many have settled on the Lordship of Christ as the most basic distinctive. Strangely, in doing this, some have attempted to separate Christ's Lordship from the authority of Scripture, as if you could embrace Christ's authority without submitting to what He commanded. However, while Christ's Lordship and Kingly authority can be isolated and considered essentially for discussion's sake, we see from Christ's own words in Luke 6:46 that His Lordship is really inseparable from His Word and, with regard to real Christian discipleship, there can be no practical submission to the one without a practical submission to the other.

In the symbol above the Kingly Crown and the Open Bible represent the inseparable truths of Christ's Kingly and Biblical authority. The Crown and Bible graphics are supplemented by three Bible verses (Ecclesiastes 8:4, Matthew 28:18-20, and Luke 6:46) that reiterate and reinforce the inextricable connection between the authority of Christ as King and the authority of His Word. The truths symbolized by these components are further emphasized by the Latin quotation - *quod scriptura, non iubet vetat*— *i.e.,* "What is not commanded in scripture, is forbidden:' This Latin quote has been considered historically as a summary statement of the regulative principle of Scripture. Together these various symbolic components converge to exhibit the two most foundational Baptist Distinctives out of which all the other Baptist Distinctives arise. Consequently, we have chosen this composite symbol as a logo to represent the primary truths set forth in the *Baptist Distinctives Series*.

THE
ACT OF BAPTISM

HENRY S. BURRAGE
1837-1926

THE ACT OF BAPTISM

IN THE

HISTORY OF THE CHRISTIAN CHURCH.

BY

HENRY S. BURRAGE.

With a Biographical Sketch of the Author by John Franklin Jones

PHILADELPHIA:
AMERICAN BAPTIST PUBLICATION SOCIETY,
1420 CHESTNUT STREET.
1879

The Baptist Standard Bearer, Inc.
NUMBER ONE IRON OAKS DRIVE • PARIS, ARKANSAS 72855

Thou hast given a *standard* to them that fear thee;
that it may be displayed because of the truth.
— Psalm 60:4

Reprinted 2006

by

THE BAPTIST STANDARD BEARER, INC.
No. 1 Iron Oaks Drive
Paris, Arkansas 72855
(479) 963-3831

THE WALDENSIAN EMBLEM
lux lucet in tenebris
"The Light Shineth in the Darkness"

ISBN# 1579784186

To the Memory

OF

HORATIO BALCH HACKETT, D.D., LL.D.,

AT WHOSE FEET AT NEWTON IT WAS MY PRIVILEGE
TO SIT,

AND WHOSE INSTRUCTIONS HAVE BEEN AN INSPIRATION
TO ME IN SUBSEQUENT YEARS,

THIS VOLUME

IS

AFFECTIONATELY DEDICATED

BY THE AUTHOR.

PREFACE.

In this volume I have endeavored to show what has been the act of baptism in the history of the Christian Church. A large number of works have been consulted in its preparation. Especially worthy of mention are the following: *Baptism, and the Baptisteries of Italy*, American Baptist Publication Society, Philadelphia, 1875, and *The Archæology of Baptism*, London, 1876, by Wolfred Nelson Cote; *Geschichtliche Darstellung der Verrichtung der Taufe*, von Dr. F. Brenner, Bamberg, 1818; *A History of the Modes of Christian Baptism*, by Rev. James Chrystal, Philadelphia, 1861; *Denkwürdigkeiten aus der Christlichen Archäologie*, von Dr. Johann Christian Wilhelm Augusti, Bd. vii., Leipzig, 1825; *The Meaning and Use of "Baptizein,"* by T. J. Conant, D. D., New York, 1868; *The History of Infant Baptism*, by W. Wall, London, 1819; *The History of Baptism*, by R. Robinson, London, 1790; *Das Sacrament der Taufe*, von Joh. Wilh. Friedrich Höfling, Erlangen, 1859; *Hippolytus and his Age*, by C. C. J. Bunsen, London, 1852; *The Creeds of Christendom*, by Philip Schaff, D. D., LL.D., New York, 1877; *The History of the English Baptists*, by Thomas Crosby, London, 1738;

PREFACE.

Bye-Paths in Baptist History, by Rev. J. Jackson Goadby, New York; *Historical Vindications,* by Sewall S. Cutting, Boston, 1859; *Geschichte der Taufe und Taufgesinnten,* von Johann August Starck, Leipzig, 1789; *Mittheilungen aus dem Antiquariate,* von Calvary & Co., Berlin, 1870; and *Johannes Kessler's Sabbata,* St. Gallen, 1870.

I should have found very helpful *The Baptism of the Ages and of the Nations,* by William Cathcart, D. D., published by the American Baptist Publication Society, Philadelphia, during the present year, had I not completed the preparation of my manuscript before the appearance of that excellent work. I find in it a few testimonies that had escaped my notice, and these I have transferred to my own pages.

For the use of some of the books mentioned above I am indebted to the library of the Newton Theological Institution, and to the library of Colby University. For valuable aid I am also indebted to the Rev. Alvah Hovey, D. D., President of the Newton Theological Institution, and especially to the Rev. Edward W. Pride of Boston, who has consulted for me rare works in the libraries of that city.

If there are other testimonies which should have a place in this attempt to show what has been the act of baptism in the history of the Christian Church, they are not purposely omitted, and I know of none that would in any way modify the general conclusions reached.

PORTLAND, Maine, Sept., 1878.

CONTENTS.

CHAPTER I.
BAPTISM IN THE NEW TESTAMENT PERIOD, A. D. 26–100 9

CHAPTER II.
FROM THE NEW TESTAMENT PERIOD TO THE COUNCIL OF NICÆA, A. D. 100–325 38

CHAPTER III.
FROM THE COUNCIL OF NICÆA TO THE COUNCIL OF TOLEDO, A. D. 325–633 53

CHAPTER IV.
FROM THE COUNCIL OF TOLEDO TO THE COUNCIL OF RAVENNA, A. D. 633–1311 91

CHAPTER V.
FROM THE COUNCIL OF RAVENNA TO THE WESTMINSTER ASSEMBLY, A. D. 1311–1644 124

CHAPTER VI.
FROM THE WESTMINSTER ASSEMBLY TO THE PRESENT TIME, A. D. 1644–1879 169

NOTES 215
INDEX 247

THE ACT OF BAPTISM.

CHAPTER I.

BAPTISM IN THE NEW TESTAMENT PERIOD.
A. D. 26–100.

It has been claimed (Lightfoot, Bengel, Wall, and others) that when John the Baptist appeared, baptism had long been in use among the Jews as an initiatory rite in the case of proselytes. There is, however, no reference to such an initiatory rite in the Old Testament. Proselytes are mentioned, but all the Old Testament writers are silent concerning proselyte baptism. The same is true of the Apocryphal books and of the books of the New Testament. Moreover, writers like Josephus and Philo make no mention of proselyte baptism. The former, as is well known, is especially minute in his allusions to the customs of the Jews; and though in several instances he refers to persons who embraced the Jewish religion and submitted to circumcision, he makes no allusion to their baptism. So also in the Mishna, or text of the Talmud, which belongs to the early part of the third century, there is no mention of proselyte baptism. The same is true of the writings of the Christian Fathers during the first four centuries. Accordingly, Meyer, in his *Commentary on Matthew* (Ger. ed., s. 97), says: "The baptism of John has been viewed wrongly as a modified application of Jewish proselyte baptism, which first came into practice after the destruction of Jerusalem. The oldest witness concerning it appears in the *Gemara Babyl. Jebamoth*, 46.2, while Philo, Josephus, and the older Targums are entirely silent in reference to such a rite." The following is from Godet's *Commentary on Luke* (Eng. ed., vol. i., p. 172): "The rite of baptism, which consisted in the plunging of the body more or less completely into water, was not at this period in use among the Jews, neither for the Jews themselves, for whom the law only prescribed lustrations, nor for proselytes from paganism, to whom, according to the testimony of history, baptism was not applied until after the fall of Jerusalem. The very title *Baptist*, given to John, sufficiently proves that it was he who introduced the rite. This follows from John i. 25, where the deputation from the Sanhedrin asks him by what right he baptizes if he is neither the Messiah nor one of the prophets, which implies that this rite was introduced by him, and further from John iii. 26, where the disciples of John make it a charge against Jesus that he adopted a ceremony of which the institution, and consequently, according to them, the monopoly, belonged to their Master." Geikie, in his *Life and Words of Christ* (Am. ed., vol. i., pp. 394, 395), states the fact thus: "With the call to repent John united a significant rite for all who were willing to own their sins and promise amendment of life. It was the new and striking requirement of baptism, which John had been sent by divine appointment to introduce. The Mosaic ritual had indeed required washings and purifications, but they were mostly personal acts for cleansing from ceremonial defilements, and were repeated as often as new uncleanness demanded. But baptism was performed only once, and those who sought it had to receive it from the hands of John. The old rites and requirements of the Pharisees would not content him. A new symbol was needed, striking enough to express the vastness of the change he demanded and to form its fit beginning, and yet simple enough to be easily applied to the whole people, for all alike needed to break with the past and to enter on the life of spiritual effort he proclaimed. Washing had, in all ages, been used as a religious symbol and a significant rite. Naaman's leprosy had been cleansed away in the waters of the Jordan. The priests in the temple practised constant ablutions, and others were required daily from the people at large to remove ceremonial impurity. David had prayed, 'Wash me from mine iniquity.' Isaiah had cried, 'Wash ye, make you clean, put away the evil of your doings.' Ezekiel had told his countrymen to 'wash their hearts from wickedness.' Ablution in the East is, indeed, of itself almost a religious duty. The dust and heat weigh upon the spirits and heart like a load. Its removal is refreshment and happiness. It was, hence, impossible to see a convert go down into a stream travel-worn and soiled with dust, and after disappearing for a moment emerge pure and fresh, without feeling that the symbol suited and interpreted a strong craving of the human heart. It was no formal rite with John."[1]

It should be added, however, that whatever difference of opinion has existed concerning the origin of proselyte baptism, there has been but

THE ACT OF BAPTISM. 13

one opinion concerning the manner in which it was administered. This was by immersion. Such is the testimony of the *Babylonian Gemara*. Maimonides, who wrote in the twelfth century, says: "There must be water sufficient for the dipping of the whole body of a man at once; and such the wise men reckon to be a cubit square and three cubits in depth." And such is the practice in the case of proselytes at the present time. Leo of Modena, Rabbi of Venice, in his book *De Ritibus et Usis Judæorum* (pars. i., c. 3), says: "He who desires to become a Jew is first circumcised, and a few days after is entirely bathed in water in presence of three rabbis who have examined him. He is then considered a Jew like the others."

The following references to baptism are found in the New Testament.

John's Baptism in General.

Matt. iii. 1, 2, 5, 6.—In those days came John the Baptist, preaching in the wilderness of Judæa, and saying, Repent ye: for the kingdom of heaven is at hand. . . . Then went out to him Jerusalem, and all Judæa, and all the region round about Jordan, and were baptized of him in Jordan, confessing their sins.

Mark i. 4, 5.—John did baptize in the wilderness, and preach the baptism of repentance for the remission of sins. And there went out unto him all the land of Judæa, and they of Jerusalem, and were all baptized of him in the river of Jordan, confessing their sins.

Luke iii. 3, 7, 8.—And he came into all the country about Jordan, preaching the baptism of repentance for the remission of sins. . . . Then said he to the multitude that came forth to be baptized of him, O generation of vipers, who hath warned you to flee from the wrath to come? Bring forth therefore fruits worthy of repentance, and begin not to say within yourselves, We have Abraham to *our* father: for I say unto you, That God is able of these stones to raise up children unto Abraham.

John i. 25-28.—And they asked him, and said unto him, Why baptizest thou then, if thou be not that Christ, nor Elias, neither that prophet? John answered them, saying, I baptize with water: but there standeth one among you, whom ye know not; he it is, who coming after me is preferred before me, whose shoe's latchet I am not worthy to unloose. These things were done in Bethabara beyond Jordan, where John was baptizing.

John iii. 23.—And John also was baptizing in

Ænon near to Salim, because there was much water there: and they came and were baptized.

Baptism of Jesus by John.

Matt. iii. 13-17.—Then cometh Jesus from Galilee to Jordan unto John, to be baptized of him. But John forbade him, saying, I have need to be baptized of thee, and comest thou to me? And Jesus answering said unto him, Suffer *it to be so* now: for thus it becometh us to fulfil all righteousness. Then he suffered him. And Jesus, when he was baptized, went up straightway out of the water: and lo, the heavens were opened unto him, and he saw the Spirit of God descending like a dove, and lighting upon him: and lo, a voice from heaven, saying, This is my beloved Son, in whom I am well pleased.

Mark i. 9-11.—And it came to pass in those days, that Jesus came from Nazareth of Galilee, and was baptized of John in Jordan. And straightway coming up out of the water, he saw the heavens opened, and the Spirit like a dove descending upon him: and there came a voice from heaven, *saying*, Thou art my beloved Son, in whom I am well pleased.

Luke iii. 21, 22.—Now when all the people were baptized, it came to pass, that Jesus also being baptized, and praying, the heaven was opened, and the Holy Ghost descended in a bodily shape like a dove upon him, and a voice came from heaven, which said, Thou art my beloved Son; in thee I am well pleased.

John i. 32–34.—And John bare record, saying, I saw the Spirit descending from heaven like a dove, and it abode upon him. And I knew him not: but he that sent me to baptize with water, the same said unto me, Upon whom thou shalt see the Spirit descending, and remaining on him, the same is he which baptizeth with the Holy Ghost. And I saw, and bare record that this is the Son of God.

OTHER REFERENCES TO BAPTISM IN THE GOSPELS.

John iii. 22.—After these things came Jesus and his disciples into the land of Judæa; and there he tarried with them, and baptized.

John iv. 1–3.—When therefore the Lord knew how the Pharisees had heard that Jesus made and baptized more disciples than John (though Jesus himself baptized not, but his disciples), he left Judæa, and departed again into Galilee.

Matt. xxviii. 18–20.—And Jesus came and spake unto them, saying, All power is given unto me in heaven and in earth. Go ye therefore, and teach all nations, baptizing them in the name of the Father, and of the Son, and of the Holy Ghost: teaching them to observe all things whatsoever I have commanded you. and lo, I am with you alway, *even* unto the end of the world. Amen.

Mark xvi. 15, 16.—And he said unto them, Go ye into all the world, and preach the gospel to every creature. He that believeth and is baptized shall be saved; but he that believeth not shall be damned.

Apostolic Baptism.

Acts ii. 37–42.—Now when they heard this, they were pricked in their heart, and said unto Peter and to the rest of the apostles, Men and brethren, what shall we do? Then Peter said unto them, Repent, and be baptized every one of you in the name of Jesus Christ for the remission of sins, and ye shall receive the gift of the Holy Ghost. For the promise is unto you, and to your children, and to all that are afar off, even as many as the Lord our God shall call. And with many other words did he testify and exhort, saying, Save yourselves from this untoward generation. Then they that gladly received his word were baptized: and the same day there were added unto them about three thousand souls. And they continued steadfastly in the apostles' doctrine and fellowship, and in breaking of bread, and in prayers.

Acts viii. 12, 13.—But when they believed Philip preaching the things concerning the kingdom of God, and the name of Jesus Christ, they were baptized, both men and women. Then Simon himself believed also ; and when he was baptized, he continued with Philip, and wondered, beholding the miracles and signs which were done.

Acts viii. 36-39.—And as they went on their way, they came unto a certain water: and the eunuch said, See, here is water: what doth hinder me to be baptized? And Philip said, If thou believest with all thine heart, thou mayest. And he answered and said, I believe that Jesus Christ is the Son of God. And he commanded the chariot to stand still: and they went down both into the water, both Philip and the eunuch; and he baptized him. And when they were come up out of the water, the Spirit of the Lord caught away Philip, that the eunuch saw him no more: and he went on his way rejoicing.

Acts ix. 17, 18.—And Ananias went his way, and entered into the house, and putting his hands on him said, Brother Saul, the Lord, even Jesus, that appeared unto thee in the way as thou camest, hath sent me, that thou mightest receive thy sight, and be filled with the Holy Ghost. And immediately there fell from his eyes as it had been scales: and he received sight forthwith, and arose, and was baptized.

Acts x. 44–48.—While Peter yet spake these words, the Holy Ghost fell on all them which heard the word. And they of the circumcision which believed were astonished, as many as came with Peter, because that on the Gentiles also was poured out the gift of the Holy Ghost. For they heard them speak with tongues, and magnify God. Then answered Peter, Can any man forbid water, that these should not be baptized, which have received the Holy Ghost as well as we? And he commanded them to be baptized in the name of the Lord. Then prayed they him to tarry certain days.

Acts xvi. 13–15.—And on the Sabbath we went out of the city by a river side, where prayer was wont to be made; and we sat down, and spake unto the women which resorted thither. And a certain woman named Lydia, a seller of purple, of the city of Thyatira, which worshipped God, heard us: whose heart the Lord opened, that she attended unto the things which were spoken of Paul. And when she was baptized, and her household, she besought us, saying, If ye have judged me to be faithful to the Lord, come into my house, and abide there. And she constrained us.

Acts xvi. 32–34.—And they spake unto him the word of the Lord, and to all that were in his house. And he took them the same hour of the night, and washed their stripes; and was baptized, he and all his, straightway. And when he had brought them into his house, he set meat before them, and rejoiced, believing in God with all his house.

Acts xviii. 8, 25.—And Crispus, the chief ruler of the synagogue, believed on the Lord with all his house; and many of the Corinthians hearing believed, and were baptized. . . . This man was instructed in the way of the Lord; and being fervent in the spirit, he spake and taught diligently the things of the Lord, knowing only the baptism of John.

Acts xix. 1–5.—And it came to pass that while Apollos was at Corinth, Paul having passed through the upper coasts came to Ephesus: and finding certain disciples, he said unto them, Have ye received the Holy Ghost since ye believed? And they said unto him, We have not so much as heard whether there be any Holy Ghost. And he said unto them, Unto what then were ye baptized? And they said, Unto John's baptism. Then said Paul, John verily baptized with the baptism of repentance, saying unto the people, that they should believe on him which should come after him, that is, on Christ Jesus. When they heard this, they were baptized in the name of the Lord Jesus.

Acts xxii. 16.—And now why tarriest thou? arise, and be baptized, and wash away thy sins, calling on the name of the Lord.

Rom. vi. 3-5.—Know ye not, that so many of us as were baptized into Jesus Christ were baptized into his death? Therefore we are buried with him by baptism into death; that like as Christ was raised up from the dead by the glory of the Father, even so we also should walk in newness of life. For if we have been planted together in the likeness of his death, we shall be also in the likeness of his resurrection.

1 Cor. i. 13-16.—Is Christ divided? was Paul crucified for you? or were ye baptized in the name of Paul? I thank God that I baptized none of you, but Crispus and Gaius; lest any should say that I had baptized in mine own name. And I baptized also the household of Stephanas; besides, I know not whether I baptized any other.

1 Cor. x. 2.—And were all baptized unto Moses in the cloud and in the sea.

Gal. iii. 27.—For as many of you as have been baptized into Christ have put on Christ.

Eph. iv. 5.—One Lord, one faith, one baptism.

Col. ii. 12.—Buried with him in baptism, wherein also ye are risen with him through the faith of the operation of God, who hath raised him from the dead.

1 Pet. iii. 20, 21.—Which sometime were disobedient, when once the long-suffering of God waited in the days of Noah, while the ark was a preparing, wherein few, that is, eight souls were saved by water. The like figure whereunto even baptism doth also now save us (not the putting away of the filth of the flesh, but the answer of a good conscience toward God), by the resurrection of Jesus Christ.

REMARKS.

In the passages which refer to the baptism of John, three places, it will be noticed, are mentioned as the scene of the forerunner's labors. 1. There was the place—probably the lower ford of the Jordan—which was most accessible to those "from Jerusalem and all Judea" who repaired to John for baptism. 2. There was Bethabara, or more properly Bethany, on the east side of the Jordan, the site of which is unknown. On Kiepert's map its location is given as opposite to Jericho. Stanley thinks it must have been on one of the upper fords of the Jordan, near Succoth, and about thirty miles from Jericho. 3. Then there was Ænon, near Salim, which, according to Jerome's testimony, was still farther north, and eight miles south of Scythopolis.

C. R. Conder, of the British Royal Engineers, and officer in charge of the survey expedition of the Palestine Exploration Fund, in his *Tent-work in Palestine* (vol. i., pp. 91, 92), places the probable site of Ænon in the valley through which Jacob drove his flocks and herds from Succoth to Shalem, near Shechem. He says:

"The head-springs are found in an open valley surrounded by desolate and shapeless hills. The water rushes out over a stony bed, and flows rapidly down in a fine stream surrounded by bushes of oleander. The supply is perennial, and a continual succession of little springs occurs along the bed of the valley, so that the current becomes the principal western affluent of the Jordan south of the well of Jezreel. The valley is open in most parts of its course, and we find the two requisites for the scene of the baptism of a huge multitude—an open space and abundance of water.

"Not only does the name Salem occur in the village three miles south of the valley, but the name Ænon, signifying 'springs,' is recognizable at the village of 'Ainun, four miles north of the stream. There is only one other place of the latter name in Palestine, Beit 'Ainun, near Hebron, but this is a place which has no very fine supply of water, and no Salem near it. On the other hand, there are many Salems all over Palestine, but none of them have an Ænon near them. The site of Wady Farah is the only spot where all the requisitions are met—the two names, the fine water-supply, the proximity of the desert, and the open character of the ground."

Ffoulkes (Smith's *Bib. Dict.*, Am. ed., vol. ii., p. 1457) suggests that John's first baptisms were at the lower ford of the Jordan, the second at Bethany, and the third at Ænon; that thus he "moved upward gradually toward Galilee, the seat of Herod's jurisdiction, by whom he was destined to be apprehended and executed."

Concerning the place of the Saviour's baptism, we only know that it was in the river Jordan. Some think that it was at the spot where the river was crossed by the Israelites under Joshua. Thus Lightfoot says: "There is reason to believe that John was baptizing in the very place where the Israelites passed over, and that our Lord was baptized in that spot where the ark rested in the bed of the river." Others think that the place was farther north. Stanley (*Sinai and Palestine*, p. 304) says that Bethabara was the scene of the Saviour's baptism. But, as Dr. Hackett has suggested (*Bib. Sacra*, July, 1866, p. 520), "for this purpose he must, contrary to the evidence, make the wilderness of Judea lie in part on the east of Jordan."

THE ACT OF BAPTISM. 25

Now from these New Testament passages what do we learn in reference to the act of baptism? First of all, the meaning and use of the word which the sacred writers employ to designate the act show that it was immersion. The evidence need not here be presented. It will be found in Conant's *Meaning and Use of Baptizein*, which is an exhaustive examination of examples of the lexical and grammatical use of the word "drawn from writers in almost every department of literature and science; from poets, rhetoricians, philosophers, critics, historians, geographers; from writers on husbandry, on medicine, on natural history, on grammar, on theology; from almost every form and style of composition—romances, epistles, orations, fables, odes, epigrams, sermons, narratives; from writers of various nations and religions, Pagan, Jew, and Christian, belonging to many different countries, and through a long succession of ages." The following paragraphs (pp. 87, 88) embody the facts derived from this extended examination.

"The ground-idea expressed by this word is *to put into* or *under water* (or other penetrable substance), so as entirely *to immerse* or *submerge;* that this act is always expressed in the literal application of the word, and is the basis of its metaphorical uses. This ground-idea is expressed in English, in the various connections where the word occurs, by the terms (synonymous in this ground-element) *to immerse, immerge, submerge, to dip, to plunge, to imbathe, to whelm.*

"The word has retained its ground-meaning without

change. From the earliest age of Greek literature down to its close (a period of about two thousand years), not an example has been found in which the word has any other meaning. There is no instance in which it signifies to make a partial application of water by *affusion* or *sprinkling*, or *to cleanse, to purify*, apart from the literal act of immersion as the *means* of cleansing or purifying."

This is the view of the best lexicographers. Liddell and Scott, in their English-Greek Lexicon, sixth English edition, revised and enlarged, give the meaning of *baptizein* as follows: [2]

"I. *To dip in or under water, to bathe*—metaphorically, *of the crowds who flocked into Jerusalem at the time of the siege;* of a man *soaked in wine, over head and ears in debt, dunned with questions.* II. *To draw wine* from bowls in cups (of course by *dipping* them). III. In the New Testament, *to baptize*." [3]

Wilke's *Lexicon of New Testament Greek*, revised and edited by C. L. W. Grimm, 1868, now in process of translation by Prof. J. H. Thayer of the Andover Theological Seminary, gives the following definition of *baptizein:*

"I. 1. *To immerse repeatedly, to immerse, to submerge;* 2. *To bathe, lave, cleanse with water by immersion or submersion.* II. (*a*) Absolutely, *to administer the rite of holy bathing, to baptize;* Vulgate, *tingo;* (*b*) with prepositions: (1) *eis*, denoting the *material* into which one is immersed (Mark i. 9), the *end* (Matt. iii. 11), the *effect* (1 Cor. xii. 13); (2) *en*, with the dative, of the substance

THE ACT OF BAPTISM. 27

into which one is immersed (Mark i. 5; John i. 31), of that with which any one baptizes (Matt. iii. 11); or with the simple dative (Luke iii. 16), to imbue largely with the Holy Spirit (Matt. iii. 11); (3) for the dead, etc. But this baptism is described as an 'immersion in water.' *Baptisma* is said to be a word peculiar to the New Testament and the church, and is defined *immersion, submersion*—(1) of calamities and afflictions by which one is overwhelmed; (2) of John's baptism; (3) of Christian baptism, and this, according to the apostolic idea, is the rite of holy submersion commanded by Christ." [4]

Prof. E. A. Sophocles of Harvard College, a Greek by birth, in his *Lexicon of Greek Usage in the Roman and Byzantine Periods* (B. C. 146–A. D. 1100), defines *baptizein* thus:

"1. *To dip, to immerse, to sink.* Tropically, *to afflict;* of a man, *soaked in liquor,* intoxicated. 2. Middle, *to perform ablution, to bathe.* 3. *To plunge* a knife. 4. *To baptize.*" "There is no evidence," he says, "that Luke and John, Paul and the other writers of the New Testament, put upon this verb meanings not recognized by the Greeks." [5]

Cremer, in his *Biblico-Theological Lexicon of New Testament Greek* (second, greatly enlarged and improved, edition, Gotha, 1872), has the following definition of *baptizein:*

"I. *To immerse, submerge,*" and he adds that the New Testament use of the word denotes "immersion, submersion for a religious purpose." [6]

THE ACT OF BAPTISM.

Added words in the Scripture record confirm this testimony from the use of *baptizein*. The believer was *buried* with Christ in baptism. Col. ii. 12. The administrator and the candidate went *down into* the water, and came up out of the water. Acts viii. 38, 39. Baptism was not *with*, but *in*, water, in the Jordan. Matt. iii. 11; Mark i. 9, etc.

Hence the following testimony of the best exegetical scholars:

Meyer, in his note on Matt. iii. 6, says: "The thing visibly and sensibly symbolized in John's baptism was the repentance. But the immersion of the entire person alone answered to this, because repentance should concern and purify the entire man, to which also afterward was connected by inner necessity the specific Christian conception of the symbolical immersion and emersion. Rom. vi. 3, *sq.;* Tit. iii. 5."

Lange, in his note on the same passage, says: "And were baptized, immersed, in the Jordan, confessing their sins."

Alford has a like note on this passage. He says: "The baptism was administered in the daytime, by immersion of the whole person."

Olshausen, in a note to his remarks on John's teaching and baptism (*Com.*, vol. i., p. 257), says: "John's baptism was most probably like the Christian, not only in this—that in it the baptizing party performed the immersion on the baptized—but that a formula was used at the immersion."

Prof. E. H. Plumptre, in Ellicott's *Commentary on*

the New Testament, in his note on Matt. iii. 11, where he considers the "baptism with the Holy Ghost," says: "As heard and understood at the time, the baptism with the Holy Ghost would imply that the souls thus baptized would be plunged, as it were, in that creative and informing Spirit which was the source of life and holiness and wisdom."

In his note on Mark vii. 4, Meyer says: "*Except they wash* is not to be understood of washing the hands (Lightfoot, Wetstein), but of immersion, which the word in classic Greek and in the New Testament everywhere means (compare Beza)—*i. e.*, here, according to the context, to take a bath. See also Luke xi. 38."

Prof. Plumptre, in his note on the same passage, says: "The Greek verb (that for *wash*) differs from that in the previous verse, and implies the washing or immersion (the verb is that from which our word *baptize* comes to us) of the whole body, as the former does of a part."

Of Luke xi. 38 he says: "Here the word *washed* (literally, though of course not in the technical sense, *baptized*) implies actual immersion, or at least a process that took in the whole body." Of Luke xii. 50 he says: "The baptism of which our Lord now speaks is that of one who is come into deep waters, so that the floods pass over him, over whose head have passed and are passing the waves and billows of many and great sorrows."

In a note to his remarks on Acts xvi. 34, 35, Meyer

says: "Immersion was a thoroughly essential part of the symbolism of baptism."

In his note on Rom. vi. 4 he says: "The recipient—thus Paul figuratively represented the process—is conscious—(*a*) in the baptism generally: 'Now am I entering into fellowship with the death of Christ;' (*b*) in the immersion in particular: 'Now am I becoming buried with Christ;' (*c*) and then, in the emergence: 'Now I rise to the new life with Christ.'"

De Wette, in his note on the same passage, says: "The death of Jesus, according to verse 10, was on account of sin, which in him was atoned for, and withal destroyed. Through an appropriation of the same by faith in baptism the power of sin in believers also is broken and the old man slain. This thought connects itself with a symbolical signification of baptism (not the original, which was that of purification) as a figure of death, inasmuch as immersion recalls the descent into Hades, or the grave."

Tholuck, in his note on this passage, says: "For the explanation of this figurative description of the baptismal rite, it is necessary to call attention to the well-known circumstance that in the early days of the church persons, when baptized, were first plunged below, and then raised above, the water, to which practice, according to the direction of the apostle, the early Christians gave a symbolical import."

Olshausen, in his comment on the same passage, says: "In this passage also we are by no means to refer the baptism merely to their own resolutions or see in it merely a figure, in which the one half of the ancient baptismal rite, the *submersion*, merely prefigures the death and burial of the old man, the second half, the *emersion*, the resurrection of the new man; we are rather to take baptism in its interior and spiritual character, as a process in the soul."

Fritsche, in his note on Matt. iii. 6, says: "That baptism was performed, not by sprinkling, but by immersion, is evident not only from the nature of the word, but from Rom. vi. 4."

Macknight, in his note on Rom. vi. 4, says: "Buried together with him by baptism. Christ's baptism was not the baptism of repentance, for he never committed any sin, but, as was observed at the beginning, he submitted to be baptized—that is, to be buried under the water—by John, and to be raised out of it again, as an emblem of his future death and resurrection."

Limborch, in his examination of the same passage, says: "The apostle alludes to the manner of baptizing, not as practised at this day, which is performed by sprinkling of water, but as administered of old in the primitive church, by immersing the whole body in water, a short continuance, and a speedy emersion out of the water."

Conybeare and Howson (*Life and Epistles of St. Paul*, vol. ii., p. 169), in a note on Rom. vi. 4, say: "This passage cannot be understood unless it be borne in mind that the primitive baptism was by immersion."

32 THE ACT OF BAPTISM.

The same figure is used by the apostle in Col. ii. 12. On this passage Canon Lightfoot, one of the first as well as one of the most recent of English commentators, says: "Baptism is the grave of the old man and the birth of the new. As he sinks beneath the baptismal waters the believer buries there all his corrupt affections and past sins; as he emerges thence he rises regenerate, quickened to new hopes and a new life. This it is because it is not only the crowning act of his own faith, but also the seal of God's adoption and the earnest of God's Spirit. Thus baptism is an image of his participation both in the death and resurrection of Christ. See *Apos. Con.*, iii. 17. For this twofold image as it presents itself to St. Paul, see especially Rom. vi. 3, *et seq.*"

Bishop Ellicott, on the same passage, says: "There seems to be no reason to doubt that both here and in Rom. vi. 4 there is an allusion to the *katadusis* and *anadusis* in baptism."

In his note on Col. iii. 1, Canon Lightfoot says: "The sacrament of baptism as administered in the apostolic age involved a twofold symbolism—a death or burial and a resurrection. In the rite itself these were represented by two distinct acts—the disappearance beneath the water and the emergence from the water. But in the change typified by the rite there are two aspects of the same thing, 'like the concave and convex in a circle,' to use an old simile. The negative side, the death and burial, implies the positive side, the resurrection. Hence, the form of the apostle's resumption, 'If ye died, if then ye were raised.'"

Bishop Wilson, in his *Lectures on Colossians*, p. 219, says: "The expression 'buried with him in baptism' alludes to the ancient form of administering that sacred ordinance, still directed in our own church, except when health forbids, of the immersion or burial, so to speak, of the whole person in the water, after the example of the burial of the entire body of our Lord in the grave."

Meyer's note on Col. ii. 12 is as follows: "The immersion in baptism, in accordance with its similarity to burial, is, seeing that baptism translates into the fellowship of the death of Christ, *a burial along with* Christ. Rom. vi. Through that fellowship of death man dies to his sinful nature, so that the body of the flesh (v. 11) ceases to live, and by means of the fellowship of burial is put off. The subject who effects the joint-burial is God, as in the whole context. In the burial of Christ this joint-burial of all who confess him, as respects their sinful body, was objectively completed; but it takes place, as respects each individually and in subjective appropriation, by their baptism, prior to which the realization of that fellowship of burial was, on the part of the individual, still wanting."

With these the best church historians agree.

Schaff, in his *History of the Apostolic Church*, vol. ii., p. 256, says: "As to the outward mode of administration of the ordinance, immersion, and not sprinkling, was unquestionably the original normal form. This is shown by the very meaning of the Greek words *baptizo, baptisma, baptismos,* used to designate the rite."

Pressensé, in his *Early Years of Christianity*, p. 374, says: "Baptism, which was the sign of admission into the church, was administered by immersion. The convert was plunged beneath the water, and as he rose from it he received the laying on of hands."

Kurtz, in his *Church History*, p. 70, says: "Baptism was administered by complete immersion in the name of Christ, or else of the Triune God. Matt. xxviii. 19."

Stanley, in his *History of the Eastern Church*, p. 117, says: "There can be no question that the original form of baptism, the very meaning of the word, was complete immersion in the deep baptismal waters, and that for at least four centuries any other form was either unknown or regarded, unless in the case of dangerous illness, as an exceptional, almost a monstrous, case. To this form the Eastern Church still rigorously adheres, and the most illustrious and venerable portion of it, that of the Byzantine empire, absolutely repudiates and ignores any other mode of administration as essentially invalid. The Latin Church has wholly altered the mode, and, with the two exceptions of the cathedral of Milan and the sect of the Baptists, a few drops of water are now the Western substitute for the threefold plunge into the rushing rivers or the wide baptisteries of the East."

Döllinger, in his *History of the Church*, vol. ii., p. 294, says: "Baptism was administered by an entire immersion in water; this immersion was three times repeated, as expressive of the faith in the Trinity—a custom which was ascribed to an apostolical ordinance or to a command of Christ."

Reuss, in his *History of Christian Theology in the Apostolic Age*, vol. ii., p. 165, says: "The form in which baptism was originally administered, that of total immersion of the person in water, suggested to Paul the idea of a double parallel of baptism—viz., with the two phases of regeneration, and with the death and resurrection of Christ. The death of the old man, the burial of the Lord, and the immersion in baptism are parallel and correlative facts; and most certainly the moral renovation, the resurrection of Christ, and the emerging from the water are the same in their turn, though there is no passage in which he says this explicitly."

Guericke, in his *Church History*, vol. i., p. 100, says: "Baptism was originally administered by immersion."

Waddington, in his *Church History*, p. 27, says: "The sacraments of the primitive church were two—those of baptism and the Lord's Supper. The ceremony of immersion (the oldest form of baptism) was performed in the name of the three Persons of the Trinity."

THE ACT OF BAPTISM.

Thiersch, in his *Church History, Apostolic Age*, vol. i., p. 279, says: "Baptism was performed by immersion in the sea or in other waters."

Mosheim, in his *Ecclesiastical History*, century i., ch. iv., sect. 8, says: "The sacrament of baptism was administered in this century, without the public assemblies, in places appointed for that purpose, and was performed by immersion of the whole body."

Venema, in his *Ecclesiastical History*, vol. i., p. 138, says: "It is without controversy that baptism in the primitive church was administered by immersion into water, and not by sprinkling."

Baron Bunsen, in his *Hippolytus and his Age*, vol. iii., p. 179, says: "The apostolic church made the school the connecting-link between herself and the world. The object of this education was admission into the free society and brotherhood of the Christian community. The church adhered rigidly to the principle, as constituting the true purport of the baptism ordained by Christ, that no one can be a member of the communion of saints but by his own free act and deed, his own solemn vow made in the presence of the church. It was with this understanding that the candidate for baptism was immersed in water and admitted as a brother upon his confession of the Father, the Son, and the Holy Ghost. It understood baptism, therefore, in the exact sense of the First Epistle of St. Peter, iii. 21—not as being a mere bodily purification, but as a vow made to God with a good conscience, through faith in Jesus Christ."

THE ACT OF BAPTISM.

This testimony is well summarized in the following statement, which Rev. L. L. Paine, D. D. (Congregationalist), professor of church history in the theological seminary at Bangor, Maine, published in an article in the *Christian Mirror*, August 3, 1875. Referring to the fact that immersion was the primitive act of baptism, he says: "The testimony is ample and decisive. No matter of church history is clearer. The evidence is all one way, and all church historians of any repute agree in accepting it. We cannot claim even originality in teaching it in a Congregational seminary. And we really feel guilty of a kind of anachronism in writing an article to insist upon it. It is a point on which ancient, mediæval, and modern historians alike, Catholic and Protestant, Lutheran and Calvinist, have no controversy. And the simple reason for this unanimity is that the statements of the early Fathers are so clear, and the light shed upon these statements from the early customs of the Church is so conclusive, that no historian who cares for his reputation would dare to deny it, and no historian who is worthy of the name would wish to."

We need not long linger, therefore, to consider the testimony that the New Testament affords in reference to the act of baptism. It was immersion, and immersion only.

CHAPTER II.

FROM THE NEW TESTAMENT PERIOD TO THE COUNCIL OF NICÆA.

A. D. 100–325.

IN the eleventh chapter of the so-called Epistle of Barnabas,[7] now believed to have been written before A. D. 119, the date to which it is usually assigned, occurs the following:

"We go down into the water full of sins and pollutions, but come up out again bringing forth fruit, having in our heart the fear and hope which are in Jesus by the Spirit."[8]

The first detailed description of the act of baptism is by Justin Martyr, who wrote his first *Apology* A. D. 139. In chap. 61 he says:

"But we will also describe the manner in which we consecrated ourselves to God, having been made new by Christ, that we may not seem, by omitting this, to deal dishonestly in our exposition. As many as are convinced and believe those things that are taught and said by us to be true, and as a promise that they are able to live thus, are taught to pray and to ask of God with fasting the forgiveness of their former sins, we ourselves praying and fasting with them. Thereupon they are led by us where there is water, and are regenerated by the same method of regeneration with which we also ourselves were regenerated; for in the name of God, the Father of all and Lord, and of our Saviour Jesus Christ, and of the Holy Ghost, they then receive the bath in water."[9]

In the work called *The Shepherd*, attributed by Irenæus, Tertullian, and Origen to Hermas (mentioned by Paul in Rom. xvi. 14), but now believed by many to have been the work of an unknown writer of the middle of the second century, occurs the following in an account (b. iii., s. iv., c. 16) of an interview between Hermas and an angel who appeared to him in a vision. The tower to which reference is made is an emblem of the church:

"'Why have these stones come up from the deep, and been placed in the structure of the tower, when, long since, they had borne the just spirits?'

"'It is necessary,' replied the angel, 'for them to ascend through the water, in order that they may have rest; for they could not have entered the kingdom of God except by putting off the mortality of their former life. Hence those who were dead were sealed with the seal of the Son of God and entered into the kingdom of God. For before a man receives the name of the Son of God he is consigned to death; but when he receives this seal he is set free from death and delivered unto life. But this seal is water, into which we go down devoted to death, but come up assigned to life. Hence, also, this seal was preached to them, and they used it that they might enter into the kingdom of God.'

"'Why, then, sir, did those forty stones which had this seal already ascend with those from the deep?'

"'Because these apostles and teachers, who preached the name of the Son of God, when they died, having this faith and power, preached to those who had died before and gave them this seal. Hence they went down into the water with them, and came up again; but these [the apostles and teachers] went down alive, while those who had died before went down dead and came up alive.'"[10]

Irenæus, a disciple of Polycarp, Bishop of Lyons in 177, and still living in 197, in his work *Against Heresies* (b. iii., c. 19), says:

"Our bodies through this bath [lavacrum] have

THE ACT OF BAPTISM.

received that which leads to an incorruptible unity."

In a fragment (see Card. Mai, *Bibl. Nova Patrum*, iii. 447) Irenæus, referring to Naaman, says:

"He dipped in Jordan seven times. Not in vain in old time was Naaman, being a leper, baptized and cleansed, but for our information, who, being lepers in our sins, are cleansed by the holy water and invocation of the Lord from our old transgressions, as new-born children spiritually regenerated, as the Lord, too, saith: Except a man be born of water and of the Spirit, he cannot enter into the kingdom of heaven." [11]

Theophilus, a bishop of Antioch in the second century, in his second book, addressed to Autolycus, a learned heathen of his acquaintance, whom he would win to the Christian faith, says:

"Men receive remission of sins through the water and washing of regeneration."

Tertullian, who died about 245, in a tract *Concerning Baptism* (*De Baptismo*), written against Quintilla of Carthage, who held that "faith alone was sufficient to save men, as it did Abraham, who pleased God without any other sacrament but that of faith," has this testimony (c. 13):

"The law of immersion has been imposed, and the form has been prescribed. 'Go,' said he, 'teach the nations, immersing them in the name of the Father, and of the Son, and of the Holy Ghost.' Matt. xxviii. 19. Comparing with this law the limitation, 'Except a man be born of water and of the Spirit, he cannot enter into the kingdom of God,' we are forced to believe in the necessity of baptism. Therefore, all who believed after these words were spoken were immersed. Then, also, Paul, when he believed, was immersed. Acts ix. 18. And this is that which the Lord commanded when he deprived him of sight: 'Arise,' said he, 'and go into Damascus, and there it shall be told thee what thou must do'—that is, be immersed, which was the only thing wanting to him." [12]

So, also, in the same tract (c. 2), Tertullian says:

"With so great simplicity, without pomp, without any considerable novelty of preparation—finally, without expense—a man is let down in the water, and, while a few words are spoken, is immersed." [13]

Again, in the same tract (c. 14), he thus expresses himself:

"He (Christ) gave as his last command that

THE ACT OF BAPTISM. 43

they should immerse into the Father and the Son and the Holy Ghost, not into one person. For we are immersed not once, but thrice, at the naming of each person of the Trinity."[14]

In his *De Corona* (c. 3.) Tertullian says:

"To begin with baptism: when we are about to come to the water, we do in the church testify, under the hand of the bishop, that we renounce the devil and his pomp and his angels. Then we are thrice dipped, pledging ourselves to something more than the Lord hath prescribed in the gospel."[15]

Concerning the place of baptism, Tertullian (*De Bapt.*, c. 4) says:

"There is no difference whether one is washed in the sea or in a pool, in a river or in a fountain, in a lake or in a canal; nor is there any difference between those whom John dipped in the Jordan and those whom Peter dipped in the Tiber."[16]

The next witness is Hippolytus, Bishop of Portus, a member of the Roman presbytery, who was born in the latter part of the second century, and was put to death about the year 236. In his discourse on the *Holy Theophany*, Hippolytus, after quoting Isa. i. 16–19, says:

"Thou sawest, beloved, how the prophet foretold the cleansing of holy baptism. For he who goes down with faith into the bath of regeneration is arrayed against the evil one and on the side of Christ; he denies the enemy and confesses Christ to be God; he puts off bondage and puts on sonship; he comes up from baptism bright as the sun, flashing forth the rays of righteousness, but, greatest of all, he comes up a son of God and a fellow-heir with Christ." [17]

Origen (184–254), in his *Commentary on the Gospel of John* (t. viii.), has this reference to baptism:

"The washing of water is the symbol of the purification of a soul cleansed of all impurity of sin." [18]

In his *Commentary on the Gospel of Matthew* he says:

"We are, therefore, through this washing (λουτρὸν), buried with Christ in regeneration."

Cyprian, Bishop of Carthage, who died in 258, says in his Epistle 25:

"The Lord, after his resurrection, when sending forth his apostles, commanded and said, All power is given unto me in heaven and in earth. Go ye, therefore, and teach all nations, immersing them in the name of the Father, and of the Son, and of the Holy Ghost, teaching them to observe all things whatsoever I have commanded you." [19]

In Epistle 65 he thus quotes Galatians iii. 27:

"For if the apostle lies not when he says, 'As many of you as were immersed into Christ have put on Christ,' then truly he who was then baptized into Christ has put on Christ." [20]

In answer to a question submitted by Magnus—"Whether they are to be esteemed legitimate Christians who are not washed in the water, but only poured about?"—Cyprian, Epistle 69, says:

"You have inquired also, dearest son, what I think of those who in sickness and debility obtain the grace of God—whether they are to be accounted legitimate Christians in that they are poured upon, not washed (*non loti sunt, sed perfusi*), with the saving water. Wherein diffidence and modesty forbid me to prejudge any that he think not as he deems right and act as he thinks. I, as far as my poor ability conceiveth, account that the divine blessings can in no respect be mutilated and weakened, nor any less gift be imparted, when what is drawn from the divine bounty is accepted with the full and entire faith both of the giver and receiver. For in the saving sacrament the contagion of sin is not so washed away as in the ordinary washing of flesh is the filth of the skin and body, so that there should be need of saltpetre and other appliances, and a bath and a pool, in which the poor body may be washed and cleansed. For otherwise is the breast of the believer washed, otherwise is the mind of man cleansed, by the worthiness of faith. In the saving sacraments, when need compels and God vouchsafes his mercy, his compendious methods confer the whole benefit on believers.[21] Nor should it disturb any one that the sick seem only to be sprinkled or affused with water when they obtain the grace of the Lord, since Holy Scripture speaks. Ezek. xxxvi. 25, 26; Num. xix. 19, 20; viii. 5; xix. 9. Whence it is apparent that the sprinkling also of water has like force with the saving washing, and that when this is done in the church, where the faith both of the giver and receiver is entire, all holds good, and is consummated and perfected by the power of the Lord and the truth of faith."

The question to which the above is an answer had reference to Novatian, who about the middle of the third century, as appears from a letter written by Cornelius, Bishop of Rome, "fell into a dangerous disease, and because he was likely to die was perfused on the bed where he lay, re-

THE ACT OF BAPTISM. 47

ceived [baptism or saving grace], if, indeed, it is proper to say that such an one could receive [baptism or saving grace]." This doubt seems to have been very general. In another part of the same letter Cornelius says:

"All the clergy and a great many of the laity were against his being chosen presbyter, because it was not lawful, they said, for any one that had been perfused, as he had been, to be admitted to any office of the clergy."

In the acts of the first Nicene Council, A. D. 325, we find the following:

"He who is baptized descends, indeed, obnoxious to sins and held with the corruptions of slavery, but he ascends free from the slavery and sins, a son of God, heir—yea, co-heir—with Christ, having put on Christ, as it is written: 'As many of you as were baptized into Christ have put on Christ.'" [22]

REMARKS.

It will be seen that in the earliest of these citations, that from the so-called *Epistle of Barnabas*, the reference is plainly to immersion. This is true, also, of the passages quoted from Justin Martyr. In his minute description, written for those with whom the customs of the infant church were unfamiliar, he gives not the slightest hint that any other form of baptism was at that time practised.[23] In the *Shepherd of Hermas* and in the writings of Irenæus and Theophilus, the references are clearly to immersion as the act of baptism. Tertullian is a witness to trine immersion in the African Church—a practice that came into use evidently at the time of the controversy concerning the Trinity. Certainly the trinity of Persons in the Godhead is the reason assigned for trine immersion by Tertullian, and later by Jerome, Basil, and the *Apostolic Canons*. Scriptural authority was not claimed for it. Jerome said, "For many other things which are by tradition observed in the church have obtained authority as if they were written laws, as in the font of baptism, *ter caput mergitare*, to plunge the head thrice under." Basil said, "The Scripture says, 'Go ye, teach and baptize;' and tradition adds, 'Baptize by trine immersion.'" But the great commission is a witness against, not for, trine immersion. As Dr. Conant has shown, "To justify such a practice, the form should have been either 'in the names of,' or 'in the name of the Father, in the name of the Son, and in the name of the Holy Spirit.'" See Conant's note on Matt. xviii. 19.

The words in the citation from Tertullian's *De Corona*, "pledging ourselves to something more than the Lord hath prescribed in the gospel," have been thought by many to refer to the change from single to trine immersion. Waterland, however, finds in them a reference to the answers made in the baptismal creed, which in Tertullian's time had been considerably enlarged.

Hippolytus and Origen are also witnesses for immersion.

In Cyprian's letter to Magnus we have the first allusion in literature to perfusion, or pouring, as baptism, and no stronger testimony to show that immersion was the primitive act of baptism could be desired than is furnished by this letter. The question suggested by Magnus, it will be seen, had no reference to the validity of pouring, except in cases in which sickness seemed to render such a departure from the primitive act necessary. Baptism had come to be regarded by many as a saving ordinance, and the question accordingly was, whether if one by reason of "sickness and debility" should find it impossible to be "washed"—that is, immersed,—he would be accounted a legitimate Christian should he upon his bed be perfused "with the saving water"? The case supposed was one of necessity. Cyprian's answer, therefore, does not countenance any irregularity in baptism under other circumstances. Believing in baptismal regeneration, he believed that the sick might and should thus receive "the saving grace of God," and so was willing to sanction, in cases of necessity, what he calls *divina compendia*—a shorter way of fulfilling the divine command. On the other hand, the question which is raised by Magnus in reference to the validity of perfusion shows that the practice must have been only recently introduced.

Certainly, if the apostolic churches or the churches of the second century had practised perfusion, even in the case of the sick, Cyprian would have referred to the fact. He had no tradition even to plead in its favor. The facts, therefore, seem to warrant the following inferences:

1. That perfusion, as it first appears in history, was not regarded as scriptural baptism, but as a substitute for immersion in cases of supposed necessity.

2. That it was considered so defective, though the answer of a good conscience, that persons who in sickness had been perfused were not deemed proper persons to receive ordination.

3. That the practice of perfusion was the outgrowth of a doctrinal error.

It is worthy of remark that the Eastern creeds had their origin in the baptismal formula, and were used at the baptismal service as the candidate's confession of faith in the triune God. Thus, Eusebius, in his account of the Council of Nicæa, says that the following creed, which he laid before that assembly, he learned as a catechumen and professed at his baptism:

"We believe in one God, the Father Almighty
  Maker of all things, visible and invisible;
  And in one Lord Jesus Christ,
  The Word of God,
  God of God,
  Light of light,
  Life of life,
  The only-begotten Son,

THE ACT OF BAPTISM.

The First Born of every creature,
Begotten of God the Father before all ages,
By whom also all things were made;
Who for our salvation was made flesh and made his home among men;
And suffered,
And rose on the third day,
And ascended to the Father,
And will come again in glory to judge the quick and the dead.
[We believe] also in one Holy Ghost."

Finally, we see that the acts of the first Nicene Council are a witness to immersion.

Kurtz, in his *Church History* (Am. ed., vol. i., p. 119), confirms the result we have reached. Referring to baptism in this period, he says:

"Baptism was performed by thrice immersing, during which the formula of baptism was pronounced; sprinkling was only common in case of the sick (*baptismus clinicorum*); the water of baptism was set apart for the sacred rite."

Neander, in his *History of the Christian Religion and Church* (vol. i., p. 310), says:

"In respect to the form of baptism, it was, in conformity with the original import of the symbol, performed by immersion as a sign of entire baptism into the Holy Spirit, of being entirely penetrated by the same. It was only with the sick, where the exigency required it, that any exception was made; and in this case baptism was administered by sprinkling."

Bunsen, in his *Hippolytus and his Age* (vol. ii., pp. 158, 159), says:

"The rules and customs respecting baptism partook both of the liturgical and the constitutional character. There were, first, rules respecting the preliminary reception of a catechumen as a pupil to be admitted to instruction. Then, generally after three years, came the solemn moment when the catechumen was to profess with certain forms his faith before the congregation, and pledge himself most solemnly, in the sight of God, to be faithful to this profession of Christianity in word and life, unto death; upon which declaration he was immersed into water in the name of the Father (God), the Son (Jesus the Christ), and the Spirit (the Life-giver of the church)."

CHAPTER III.

FROM THE COUNCIL OF NICÆA TO THE COUNCIL OF TOLEDO.

A. D. 325–633.

THE first witness in this period is Athanasius (296–373 circ.), who was made Bishop of Alexandria in 328. In his *Discourse on the Holy Passover*, 5, he says:

"In these benefits thou wast baptized, O newly-enlightened; the initiation into the grace, O newly-enlightened, has become to thee an earnest of resurrection; thou hast the baptism as a surety of the abode in heaven. Thou didst imitate, in the sinking down, the burial of the Master; but thou didst rise again from thence before works, witnessing the works of the resurrection." [24]

The same writer, in his *Questions on the Psalms*, Prop. 92, says:

"For that the child sinks down thence in the font and comes up, this shows the death of Christ, and the resurrection on the third day." [25]

Another witness is Cyril (315–386), who was

made Bishop of Jerusalem in 350. The following was the order of baptism in the church in Jerusalem, as recorded by Cyril in the sermons for the instruction of the newly baptized (*Catecheses Mystag.*, 1, iii.), which he preached in the church of the Holy Sepulchre, about the year 350 or 360:

"You went first into the porch (baptistery); and being placed toward the west, you heard the command to stretch out your hands and to renounce Satan as if he were present, . . . and to say, 'I renounce Satan . . . and all his works . . . and all his pomp and all his service.' After this thou wast turned toward the east, and wast commanded to say, 'I believe in the Father, and in the Son, and in the Holy Ghost, and in a baptism of repentance.' All this was done in the porch. But when you were entered into the inner house, you took off your garment, and thus you were anointed with the holy oil from the top of the head to the sole of the feet. . . . Then you were conducted to the font of the holy baptism, and each one was asked whether he believed in the name of the Father, and the Son, and of the Holy Ghost. And you made the sound confession of faith, and were three times baptized in the water."

THE ACT OF BAPTISM. 55

The act is more fully described in the following citation from Lecture xx. *Myst.* ii. 4:

"After these things ye were led by the hand to the sacred font of divine baptism, as Christ from the cross to the prepared tomb. And each was asked if he believed in the name of the Father, and of the Son, and of the Holy Spirit, and ye professed the saving profession, and sunk down thrice into the water, and again came up, and thus, by a symbol, shadowing forth the burial of Christ," etc.[26]

Another description is contained in the following passage from Lecture xvii., on the *Holy Spirit*, ii. 14:

"For the Lord saith, 'Ye shall be baptized in the Holy Spirit not many days after this.' Not in part the grace, but all-sufficing the power! For as he who sinks down in the waters, and is baptized, is surrounded on all sides by the waters, so also they were completely baptized by the Spirit."[27]

In 348, at the Council of Carthage, in a discussion concerning rebaptism, Bishop Gratus said:

"I ask this sacred assembly to express their opinion whether, when a man has descended into the water, and has been questioned as to his belief in the Trinity, according to the faith of the gospel and the doctrine of the apostles, and has made a good confession concerning the resurrection of Jesus Christ, he ought to be again questioned concerning the same faith, and again immersed in water." [28]

And all the bishops answered, "Far be it! far be it!"

Basil (329–379), Bishop of Cesarea in Cappadocia, in his *De Spiritu Sancto* (*Opera*, vol. iv., p. 112, ed. Migne, Paris, 1857), has the following allusions to the act of baptism:

"How can we be placed in a condition of likeness to his death? By being buried with him in baptism. What is the form of this burial, and what benefits flow from an imitation of it? First, the course of former life is stopped. No man can do this unless he be born again, as the Lord hath said. Regeneration, as the word itself imports, is the beginning of a new life; therefore he who begins a new life must put an end to his former life. Such a person resembles a man at the end of a race, who, before he sets off again, turns about, pauses, and rests a little: so in a change of life it seems necessary that a sort of death should intervene, putting a period to the past and giving a beginning to the future. How are we to go down with him into the grave? By imitating the burial of Christ in baptism; for the bodies of the baptized are in a sense buried in water. For this reason the apostle speaks figuratively of baptism as laying aside the works of the flesh: Ye are circumcised with the circumcision made without hands, in putting off the body of the sins of the flesh by the circumcision of Christ, buried with him in baptism, which, in a manner, cleanses the soul from the impurity of its natural carnal affections, according as it is written, ' Wash me, and I shall be whiter than snow.' This is not like the Jewish purifications, washing after every defilement, but we have experienced it to be one cleansing baptism, one death to the world, and one resurrection from the dead; of both of which baptism is a figure. For this purpose the Lord, the Giver of life, hath instituted baptism—a representation of both life and death, the water overflowing as an image of death, the Spirit animating as an earnest of life. Thus we see that water and the Spirit are united. Two things are proposed in baptism—to put an end to a life of sin, lest it should issue in eternal death, and to animate the soul to a life of future sanctification. The water exhibits an image of death, receiving the body as into a sepulchre; the Spirit renews the soul, and we rise from a death of sin into a newness of life. This is to be born from above of water and the Spirit; as if by the water we were put to death, and by the operation of the Spirit brought to life. By three immersions, therefore, and by three invocations, we administer the important ceremony of baptism, that death may be represented in a figure, and that the souls of the baptized may be purified by divine knowledge.[29] If there be any benefit in the water, it is not from the water, but from the presence of the Spirit; for baptism does not 'save us by putting away the filth of the flesh,' but by 'the *answer of a good conscience* toward God.'"

Also, in Epistle 236 (*Opera, Epistolarum Classis II.*, vol. iv., p. 884, ed. Migne, Paris, 1857), Basil says:

"But concerning the emersion in baptism, I hardly know why it should occur to you to ask if you received immersion to fulfil the figure of the three days. For it is not possible to be immersed thrice unless one emerges as many times."[30]

Gregory of Nazianzen (328–389), in his thirty-ninth sermon, says:

"Moses truly baptized in water by causing the Israelites to pass through the sea and under the cloud. The sea represents the waters of baptism, and the cloud the Holy Spirit."

In his sermon (fortieth) on *Holy Baptism* he says:

"Let us therefore be buried with Christ through the baptism, that we may also rise with him, that we may also be exalted with him; let us come up with him that we may also be glorified with him." [31]

In his sermon *De Pœnitentia*, Gregory, Bishop of Nyssa (331–400 circ.), says:

"The old man is buried in water; the new man is born again, and grows in grace."

In his sermon *De Bapt. Christi* he says:

"We, who receive baptism in imitation of our Lord and Teacher and Guide, are not buried in the earth, for this covers the entire lifeless body and enwraps the weakness and corruption of our nature; . . . but coming to the water, the element cognate to the earth, we hide ourselves in it as the Saviour hid himself in the earth, and this we do three times to represent the grace of his resurrection performed after three days." [32]

Jerome (331–420), in his note on Eph. iv. 5, 6, says:

"We are dipped in water that the mystery of the Trinity may appear to be but one, and therefore, though we be thrice put under water to represent the mystery of the Trinity, yet it is reputed but one baptism." [33]

In a letter to Fabiola, referring to the custom of wearing white garments a week after baptism, he says:

"We are to be washed with the precepts of God; and when we are prepared for the garment of Christ, putting off our coat of skins, we shall put on the linen garment that hath nothing of death in it, but is all white, that, rising out of the waters of baptism, we may gird about our loins with truth and cover the former filthiness of our breasts." [34]

Ambrose (340–397), in his work *De Sacram.*, lib. ii., c. 7, says:

"Thou wast asked, 'Dost thou believe in God the Father almighty?' and thou repliedst, 'I believe,' and wast dipped—that is, buried. A second demand was made: 'Dost thou believe in Jesus Christ, our Lord, and in his cross?' Thou answeredst again, 'I believe,' and wast dipped. Therefore thou wast buried with Christ, for he who is buried with Christ rises again with Christ. A third time the question was repeated, 'Dost thou believe in the Holy Ghost?' and thy answer was, 'I believe.' Then thou wast dipped a third

THE ACT OF BAPTISM. 61

time, that thy triple confession might absolve thee from the various offences of thy former life." [35]

In the same chapter also he says:

"The apostle then teaches, as you have heard in the present lesson, 'so many of us as were baptized into Jesus Christ were baptized into his death.' Rom. vi. 3. What is the meaning of 'into his death'? As Christ died, so dost thou taste death. As Christ died to sin and lives to God, so thou also, by the sacrament of baptism, didst die to the snares of former sins, and thou didst rise by Christ's grace. A death there is, therefore, but not in a reality a death of the body, but only in a similitude. For when thou wast dipped thou didst undergo the similitude both of a death and burial." [36]

In lib. iii., c. 1, 1, he says:

"Yesterday we discoursed respecting the font, whose appearance is, as it were, a form of the sepulchre, into which, believing in the Father, and the Son, and the Holy Spirit, we are received and submerged, and rise—that is, are restored—to life." [37]

In lib. ii., c. 6, 19, alluding to the words, "dust thou art," etc., he says:

"Hear, then; for that in this age also the bond of the devil might be loosed, it has been found how a living man might die, and, living, rise again. What is 'living'? This is the living life of the body when it came to the font and was immersed in the font. What is water except of earth? The divine sentence is satisfied, therefore, without the stupor of death. In that thou sinkest down, that sentence is discharged, 'Earth thou art, and into earth thou shalt go.' The sentence being fulfilled, there is room for the blessing and for the divine remedy. Water, then, is of earth; but the capability of our life did not allow that we should be covered with earth and rise again from the earth. Moreover, earth does not cleanse, but water cleanses; therefore the font is as a sepulchre."[38]

Chrysostom (354–407), Bishop of Antioch, in his *Homily 25*, says:

"In this symbol [baptism] are fulfilled the pledges of our covenant with God: death and burial, resurrection and life; and these take place all at once. For when we sink our heads under the water, the old man is buried as in a tomb below and wholly sunk for ever; then, as we raise them up, the new man rises again. As it is easy for us to dip and lift our heads again, so it is easy for God to bury the old man and show forth the new; and this is done three times, that you may learn that the power of the Father, the Son, and the Holy Ghost fulfilled all this."[39]

In his *Homily* (40) *on the Epistle to the Romans* he says:

"For as his [Christ's] body, by being buried in the earth, brought forth as the fruit of it the salvation of the world, thus ours also, being buried in baptism, bare as fruit righteousness, sanctification, adoption, countless blessings; and it will bear also hereafter the gift of the resurrection. Since, then, we were buried in the water, he in the earth, we in regard to sin, he in regard to his body, this is why he [Paul] does not say, 'We were planted together in his death,' but 'in the likeness of his death.'"[40]

So also in his *Homily* (40, 1) *on 1 Corinthians* he says:

"For to be baptized and to sink down, then to emerge, is a symbol of the descent into the underworld and of the ascent from thence. Therefore Paul calls baptism a burial, saying, 'We were buried, therefore, with him by baptism into death.'"[41]

In his *Homily on Faith* he says:

"Christ delivered to his disciples one baptism in three immersions of the body when he said to them, 'Go teach all nations, baptizing them in the name of the Father, and of the Son, and of the Holy Spirit.'"[42]

Augustine (354–430), in his sermon *De Mysterio Baptismatis*, has this reference to the act of baptism, though the genuineness of the passage has by some been questioned:

"In this font, before we dipped your whole body, we asked you, 'Believest thou in God, the omnipotent Father?' . . . After you averred that you believed, we immersed three times your heads in the sacred font. For you are rightly immersed three times who receive baptism in the name of the Trinity. You are rightly immersed three times, you who receive baptism in the name of Jesus Christ, who rose the third day from the dead. Trine immersion is the symbol of the burial of the Lord, by which you are buried with Christ in baptism, and with Christ rise again by faith, that, purified of your sins, you may live, following Christ in the holiness of virtue."[45]

In his *Aurea Catena*, on Matt. iii. 13–15 he says:

"The Saviour willed to be baptized, not that he might himself be cleansed, but to cleanse the water for us. From the time that himself was dipped in the water, from that time has he washed away all our sins in water. . . . Thus the blessing, which, like a spiritual river, flows on from the Saviour's baptism, hath filled the basins of all pools and the courses of all fountains."

To this period belong the *Apostolical Constitutions*, eight books that claim to have been written by the hand of Clement of Rome, and to be the words of the apostles themselves. That they are not of apostolic origin, however, is now conceded; and all that can be said in reference to them is that they reflect views current in the churches during the fourth century. Concerning the act of baptism we find in Book iii. 15 the following:

"And at the time of the crowing of the cock let them first pray over the water. Let the water be drawn into the font, or flow into it, and let it be thus if there is no scarcity. But if there be a scarcity, let them pour the water which shall be found into the font; and let them undress themselves, and the young shall be first baptized. And all who are able to answer for themselves, let them answer. But those who are not able to answer, let their parents answer for them, or one from among their relations. And after the men have been baptized, then the women, having loosed their hair and laid aside their ornaments of gold and silver. Let no one take a strange garment with him into the water.

"And at the time which is appointed for the baptism, let the bishop give thanks over the oil, which, putting into a vessel, he shall call the oil of thanksgiving. Again, he shall take other oil; and exorcising over it, he shall call it the oil of exorcism. And a deacon shall bear the oil of exorcism and stand on the left hand of the presbyter. Another deacon shall take the oil of thanksgiving and stand on the right hand of the presbyter.

"And when the presbyter has taken hold of each one of those who are about to receive baptism, let him command him to renounce, saying, 'I renounce thee, Satan, and all thy service and all thy works.' And when he has renounced all these, let him anoint him with the oil of exorcism, saying, 'Let every spirit depart from thee!'

"And let the bishop or the presbyter receive him thus unclothed, to place him in the water of baptism. Also let the deacon go with him into the water, and let him say to him, helping him that he may say, 'I believe in the only true God, the Father almighty, and in his only begotten Son, Jesus Christ, our Lord and Saviour, and

THE ACT OF BAPTISM.

in the Holy Spirit, the Quickener; one sovereignty, one kingdom, one faith and baptism, in the holy catholic church, in the life everlasting. Amen.'

"And let him who receives [baptism] repeat after all these, 'I believe thus.' And he who bestows it shall lay his hand upon the head of him who receives, dipping him three times, confessing these things each time.

"And afterward let him say again, 'Dost thou believe in our Lord Jesus Christ, the only Son of God the Father; that he became man in a wonderful manner for us, in an incomprehensible unity, by his Holy Spirit, of Mary, the holy Virgin, without the seed of man; and that he was crucified for us under Pontius Pilate, died of his own free will once for our redemption, rose on the third day, loosened the bonds [of death]; he ascended up into heaven, sat on the right hand of his good Father on high, and he cometh again to judge the living and the dead at his appearing and his kingdom? And dost thou believe in the holy good Spirit and Quickener, who wholly purifieth, and in the holy church?'

"Let him again say, 'I believe.'

"And let them go up out of the water, and the presbyter shall anoint him with the oil of thanksgiving, saying, 'I anoint thee with the holy anointing oil in the name of Jesus Christ.' Thus he shall anoint all of the rest, and clothe them as the rest, and they shall enter into the church.

"Let the bishop lay his hand upon them with affection, saying, 'Lord God, as thou hast made them worthy to receive the forgiveness of their sins in the world to come, make them worthy to be filled with thy Holy Spirit, and send upon them thy grace, that they may serve thee according to thy will, for thine is the glory of the Father, and of the Son, and of the Holy Spirit, in the holy church, now and always, and for ever and ever.' And he shall pour of the oil of thanksgiving on the hand, and put the hand upon his head, saying, 'I anoint thee with the holy anointing oil from God the Father almighty, and Jesus Christ, and the Holy Spirit.' And he shall seal upon his forehead, saluting him."

To this fourth century also, or to the early part of the fifth century, belong the so-called *Apostolic Canons*, which, about A. D. 500, Dionysius Exiguus, a Roman monk, at the request of Stephen, Bishop of Salona, collected and translated from Greek into Latin. The fiftieth canon is as follows:

"50. If any bishop or presbyter does not administer trine immersion [*trinam mersionem*] of the one initiation, but one immersion which is given into the death of Christ, let him be deposed; for the Lord did not say to us, 'Baptize into my death,' but, 'Go ye and make disciples of all nations, baptizing them into the name of the Father, and of the Son, and of the Holy Ghost.' Do ye therefore, O bishops, baptize thrice into the one Father, and Son, and Holy Ghost, according to the will of Christ, and our Constitutor by the Spirit."

The next witness is Theodoret (393–457), Bishop of Cyrus, who (*Hæret. Fabul.*, l. iv., c. 3.) says in a reference to Eunomius, from whom the heretical sect known as Eunomians took their name:

"He subverted the law of holy baptism, which had been handed down from the beginning from the Lord and the apostles, and made a contrary law, asserting that it is not necessary to immerse the candidate for baptism thrice, nor to mention the names of the Trinity, but to baptize once only into the death of Christ." "

Sozomen, the church historian, who died A. D. 450, says in his *Eccl. Hist.*, lib. vi. c. 26:

"Some say that Eunomius was the first who dared to bring forward the notion that the divine baptism ought to be administered by a single immersion, and to corrupt the tradition which has been handed down from the apostles, and which is still observed by all."⁴⁵ . . . But whether it was Eunomius, or any other person, who first introduced heretical opinions concerning baptism, it seems to me that such innovators, whoever they may have been, were alone in danger, according to their own representation, of quitting this life without having received baptism according to the ancient mode of the church; they found it impossible to reconfer it on themselves. It must be admitted that they introduced a practice to which they had not themselves submitted, and thus undertook to administer to others what had never been administered to themselves."

Leo the Great, who was elected Pope of Rome in 440, in his fourth letter to the bishops of Sicily, wrote:

"Trine immersion is an imitation of the three days' burial, and the rising again out of the water is like the rising from the grave." ⁴⁶

Maximus, Bishop of Turin, said to have died A. D. 466, in his homily *De Juda Traditore*, says:

"Baptism is to us burial with Christ, in which we die to sin and iniquity; and the old man being destroyed, we rise again to new life. It is a burial by which we lay down our life, and receive it anew that we may live. Great, therefore, is the grace of this sepulture, through which a useful death is brought to us, and a still more useful life freely bestowed. Great is the grace of this sepulture with Christ, which purifies the sinner and gives life to the dying."[47]

So, also, in his third treatise on baptism, he says:

"Here in the font man is immersed."[48]

In another passage he says:

"Before we immersed your whole body in this font, we asked, 'Dost thou believe in God, the Father almighty?' Thou answeredst, 'I believe,'" etc.[49]

Theodulus, Presbyter of Cœle-Syria, who died about A. D. 490, says in his *Commentary on the Epistle of Paul to the Romans:*

"As the body of our Lord was buried in the earth, so our body is buried by baptism. The three burials and resurrections typified by the threefold dipping symbolize his death and resurrection."[50]

Gennadius of Marseilles, a learned ecclesiastical writer, who died A. D. 492, in his *De Eccl. Dogmatibus*, c. 52, says:

"It is not to be believed that those are baptized who have not been immersed in the name of the Father, and of the Son, and of the Holy

Ghost, according to the rule established by the Lord." [51]

In the same work, c. 74, according to the MS. which Migne follows, Gennadius says:

"After confession he is either sprinkled with water or immersed, or, martyr-like, is sprinkled with blood or touched with fire." [52]

From this passage Wall argues that Gennadius regarded the mode as indifferent. But the *aspergitur*, taken in connection with the passage from c. 52, evidently refers to cases of supposed necessity.

In the baptismal liturgy of Gelasius, who was made pope A. D. 492, we find the following directions:

"On Saturday morning the children recite the creed. First catechize them, the hand placed upon their heads.

"Then touch his nostrils and ears with spittle and say to him in his ear, Ephphatha (which is, Be thou opened), in odor of sweetness. But flee away, O devil, for the judgment of God is at hand.

"Then touch his breast and between the shoulders with exorcised oil, and calling him by name say to each one:

"Dost thou renounce Satan?

"*Ans.*—I do renounce him.

"And all his works?

"*Ans.*—I do renounce them.

"And all his pomps?

"*Ans.*—I do renounce them.

"Recite the Creed with the hand placed upon their heads.

"Then the archdeacon shall say to them, 'Pray, ye elects; bow the knee. Finish your prayer at once, and say Amen.'

"And all shall answer, 'Amen.'

"The archdeacon shall again give them notice, as follows: 'Let the catechumens draw back. Let all the catechumens go out.'

"The deacon says again, 'Dearly-beloved sons, return to your places, and wait for the hour in which baptism may be operated in you by the grace of God.'

"Prayer for Holy Saturday.

"Omnipotent and eternal God, behold propitiously the devotion of thy regenerated people, who, as the hart, seek the fountain of waters, and grant that the ardor of their faith, through the mystery of baptism, sanctify both soul and body.

"Then they proceed to the fonts, chanting the litany used for baptizing."

[After this the liturgy for blessing or consecrating the font follows. Then the following questions are addressed to the candidates by the priest:]

"Believest thou in God, the almighty Father?

"*Ans.*—I do believe.

"Believest thou in Jesus Christ, his only Son, our Lord, who was born and suffered?

"*Ans.*—I do believe.

"Believest thou in the Holy Ghost, the holy church, the remission of sins, and the resurrection of the dead?

"*Ans.*—I do believe.

"Then immerse him three times in the water. When the child has come out of the font,[53] let him be signed on the head with chrism, the following words being said:

"'Almighty God, the Father of our Lord Jesus Christ, who hath regenerated thee by water and the Holy Ghost, and hath given unto thee remission of all thy sins, may he anoint thee with the chrism of salvation unto life everlasting.'

"*Ans.*—Amen."

In the second book (c. 31) of his *History of France*, Gregory of Tours designates the edifice at Rheims in which King Clovis was baptized (496) by Remigius, or Remy, Bishop of Rheims, *Tem-*

plum Baptisterii. Referring to the baptism of the king, he says:

"The news of the conversion of the Franks is carried to St. Remy, who, filled with joy, orders the sacred fonts to be immediately prepared; decorated draperies overshadow the streets; the churches are ornamented with curtains; the baptistery is put in order; clouds of perfume arise; sweet-scented tapers are burning; the entire temple of the baptistery is filled with a divine odor; and the Lord gave his grace to the assistants in such abundance that they fancied themselves surrounded by the perfumes of paradise. The king was the first to request baptism from the pontiff. Another Constantine, he advances toward the bath which is to wash away his leprosy; he comes to purify in the fresh water the hideous stains of his past life. As he is about to enter into the font, the saint of God says to him in an eloquent voice: 'Sicamber, bow humbly thy head; adore what thou hast burnt, and burn what thou hast adored.' The king, having confessed his belief in one all-powerful God in the Trinity, was baptized in the name of the Father, the Son, and the Holy Ghost, and was anointed with the holy chrism, administered with the sign of the cross of Christ; more than three thousand men of his army were also baptized, as well as his sister Albofleda, who, not long after, died in the Lord."[54]

In the liturgy that was used by Remigius at the administration of baptism occurs the following:

"The presbyters or the deacons, or, if need be, the acolyths, having put on other robes, proceed to the font and enter into the water; and receiving them from their parents, baptize, first the males and then the females, by trine immersion, with but one invocation of the Holy Trinity, saying, 'I baptize thee in the name of the Father (and dip once), and of the Son (and dip again), and of the Holy Spirit' (and dip the third time).[55]

"When they have come out of the font, the presbyter dips his thumb in the chrism and anoints them on the crown of the head in the form of the cross, saying, 'Almighty God, the Father of our Lord Jesus Christ,' etc.

"They are then received by the sponsors, and the pontiff walks out of the font and takes his seat in the church. The children are brought to him, and he gives them a stole, a chasuble, the chrism, and ten silicas, and then the children are clothed. They afterward attend mass, and they are recommended not to take any food till after they have received the communion."

Pope Pelagius, who died A. D. 560, says:

"There are many who say that they baptize in the name of Christ alone and by a single immersion. But the gospel command, which was given by God himself and our Lord and Saviour Jesus Christ, reminds us that we should administer holy baptism to every one in the name of the Trinity and by trine immersion, for our Lord said to his disciples, 'Go baptize all nations in the name of the Father, and of the Son, and of the Holy Spirit.'" [56]

Gregory, Presbyter of Antioch (570–593), in his *De Baptismo Christi*, Sermon 1, represents Christ as saying to John at his baptism:

"Cover me in the floods of the Jordan, as she who bore me wrapped me in the clothes of infancy." [57]

Gregory, known in history as Gregory the Great, born about the year A. D. 540, elected pope in 590, and who died in 604, was the author of great alterations in the ceremonials of the Roman Church, but he made no attempt to introduce any change in reference to the act of baptism. In his *Sacramentary* we find the following:

"Let the priest baptize with a triple immersion,

but with only one invocation of the Holy Trinity, saying, 'I baptize thee in the name of the Father (then let him immerse the person once), and of the Son (then immerse him a second time), and of the Holy Spirit' (and immerse him a third time."[58]

But while this was the practice at Rome, Gregory sanctioned single immersion in Spain. Certain bishops of that country asked his advice. They practised single immersion, they said, in opposition to the Arians among them, who claimed that in trine immersion the Son and the Holy Spirit were recognized as holding a subordinate position to the Father, inasmuch as immersion in the name of the Father preceded that in the name of the Son and of the Holy Spirit. One immersion, it was thought, in the name of the Father, Son, and Holy Spirit, would fitly represent the equality of the members of the Trinity. In a letter to Leander, Bishop of Seville, in answer to this request for advice, Gregory said:

"Concerning the three immersions in baptism, you have judged very truly already that different customs do not prejudice the holy church whilst the unity of the faith remains entire. The reason why we use three immersions is to signify the mystery of Christ's three days' burial, that, whilst an infant is thrice lifted up out of the water, the resurrection on the third day may be expressed thereby. But if any one thinks it is rather done in regard to the holy Trinity, a single immersion in baptism does in no way prejudice that; for so long as the unity of the substance is preserved in three persons, it is no harm whether a child be baptized with one immersion or three, because three immersions may represent the trinity of Persons and one immersion the unity of Godhead. But forasmuch as heretics now baptize the infant with three immersions, I think you ought not to do so, lest the immersions be interpreted as a division of the Godhead."[59]

In his *Historia Ecclesiastica Gentis Anglorum* (lib. ii., c. 14), the Venerable Bede, who died A. D. 735, has the following account of the baptism of King Edwin by Paulinus at York, England, in 627:

"King Edwin, with all the nobility of the nation and a large number of the people, received the faith and the washing of the holy regeneration in the eleventh year of his reign, which is the year of the incarnation of our Lord six hundred and twenty-seven. He was baptized at York on the holy day of Easter, being the 12th of April, in the church of St. Peter the Apostle, which he himself had built of timber whilst he was being catechized and instructed in order to receive baptism. . . . So great was then the fervor of the faith, as is reported, and the desire of the washing of salvation among the nation of the Northumbrians, that Paulinus, at a certain time coming with the king and queen to the royal villa, called Adgefrin, stayed there with them thirty-six days, fully occupied in catechizing and baptizing; during which days, from morning till night, he did nothing else but instruct the people, resorting from all villages and places, in Christ's saving word; and when instructed, he washed them with the water of absolution in the river Glen. . . . These things happened in the province of the Berniclans; but in that of Deiri also, where he was wont often to be with the king, he baptized in the river Swale, which runs by the river Cataract; for as yet oratories or baptisteries could not be made in the early infancy of the church in those parts."[60]

The advice of Gregory the Great, in which he gave his sanction to the practice of single immersion in Spain, as contained in his letter to the bishop of Seville, was confirmed by the fourth Council of Toledo in 633, which decreed that it is not necessary to immerse the candidate three times, and that a single immersion is sufficient.[61]

REMARKS.

It is evident from these citations that throughout this period trine immersion was the rule in the Christian Church. Single immersion was practised only by the Eunomians, and, during the latter part of the period, by the churches in Spain under the sanction of Pope Gregory the Great.

Bingham, in his *Antiquities of the Christian Church* (London, 1840, vol. iii., bk. xi., chap. xi., pp. 604–606), states the case thus:

"The Arians in Spain, not being of the sect of the Eunomians, continued for many years to baptize with three immersions; but then they abused this ceremony to a very perverse end—to patronize their error about the Son and Holy Ghost's being of a different nature or essence from the Father; for they made the three immersions to denote a difference or degrees of diversity in the three divine Persons. To oppose whose wicked doctrine, and that they might not seem to symbolize with them in any practice that might give encouragement to it, some Catholics began to leave off the trine immersion as savoring of Arianism, and took up the single immersion in opposition to them. But this was like to prove a matter of scandal and schism among the Catholics themselves; and therefore, in the time of Gregory the Great, Leander, Bishop of Seville, wrote to

F

him for his advice and resolution in this case. . . . Yet this judgment of Pope Gregory did not satisfy all men in the Spanish Church, for still many kept to the old way of baptizing by three immersions, notwithstanding this fear of symbolizing with the Arians. Therefore, some time after, about the year 633, the fourth Council of Toledo, which was a general council of all Spain, was forced to make another decree to determine this matter and settle the peace of the church. For while some priests baptized with three immersions, and the others with but one, a schism was raised, endangering the unity of the faith; for the contending parties carried the matter so high as to pretend that they who were baptized in a way contrary to their own were not baptized at all. To remedy which evil, the Fathers of this council first repeat the judgment of Pope Gregory, and then immediately conclude upon that, though both these ways of baptism were just and unblamable in themselves, according to the opinion of that great man, yet, as well to avoid the scandal of schism as the usage of heretics, they decree that only one immersion should be used in baptism, lest if any used three immersions they might seem to approve the opinion of heretics, whilst they followed their practice. And that no one might be dubious about the use of a single immersion, he might consider that the death and resurrection of Christ were represented by it. For the immersion in water was, as it were, the descending into hell, or the grave, and the emersion out of the water was a resurrection

He might also observe the unity of the Deity and the trinity of Persons to be signified by it—the unity by a single immersion, and the trinity by giving baptism in the name of the Father, Son, and Holy Ghost."

Clinic baptism was continued, and in cases of necessity aspersion or affusion was undoubtedly often, though not always, practised. Gennadius, however, is the only witness for aspersion in this period, so far as we are aware, and Brenner (*Geschichtliche Darstellung d. Verrichtung d. Taufe*, s. 15) claims that its use was extraordinary, and only when necessity compelled. The prejudice against clinic baptism, indeed, was such that only in exceptional cases was a clinic considered as qualified for ordination. The Council of Neo-Cesarea, A. D. 350, in Canon 12, decreed:

"If any man has been baptized in sickness, he must not be promoted to be a presbyter, for his faith was not of his own free choice, but of necessity—unless, perhaps, an exception is made on account of his subsequent diligence and faith, or on account of a scarcity of men."

The general feeling at that time in reference to clinics also finds expression in the following words of Chrysostom, who in one of his homilies places in contrast those to whom baptism had been regularly administered and those who had received clinic baptism:

"They receive their baptism lying upon their beds, you receive it in the bosom of the church, which is the mother of all the faithful; they receive it weeping, and you with joy; they with groans, and you with thanksgiving; they in the heat of a fever, and you under the sense of the heavenly grace. Everything here has a relation to the grace received, there everything disagrees with it; there are sighings and tears while the sacrament is administered; children cry, the wife tears her hair, friends are dejected, servants weep, the whole house is in mourning; and if you consider the spirit of the sick person, you shall find it more full of sorrow than that of the bystanders; for as a stormy sea divides into several waves, so his soul, being agitated by troubles, is torn by a thousand disquiets and racked with infinite troubles."

It has been urged by some that, while immersion was the rule during this period, there are not wanting in art indications of the practice of aspersion or affusion in other cases than those of clinics. An appeal is made to the fresco in the catacomb of St. Calixtus, and also to the representation of the baptism of Christ in one of the mosaics in the cupola of the celebrated baptistery at Ravenna. But as no reference to such a usage is to be found in the literature of the period, those who find aspersion in these representations are obliged, on a review of the evidence (see, for example, Smith's *Dictionary of Christian Antiquities*, Eng. ed., vol. i., p. 169), to adopt the suggestion that the two modes were at that time combined, as at the present day in the Armenian order of baptism, which requires that the priest shall first bury the child, or catechumen, thrice in the water, as a figure of Christ's three days' burial, and then, taking the child out of the water, shall thrice pour a handful of water on its head.

But in reference to these early representations of baptism, Roman writers are by no means agreed that they are witnesses for aspersion or affusion in the period to which they are commonly assigned. Thus, concerning the fresco in the catacomb of St. Calixtus, Father Garrucci, in his illustrated work on the *History of Christian Art* (vol. ii., p. 12), maintains that it is not a representation of baptism by affusion. In his description of the picture he says: "The youth, entirely naked, is entirely immersed in a cloud of water." [62]

In the mosaic representation of the baptism of Christ in the cupola of the baptistery at Ravenna, Christ is seen standing up to his waist in the Jordan, while John is pouring water upon his head from a cup. But it should be borne in mind that the head of the Saviour and the right arm of John have been restored, and that it is the opinion of competent critics that we are indebted to the restorer for the cup which John now holds in his uplifted hand. Hence these words of Crowe and Calvacasella in reference to the Ravenna mosaics in their *History of Painting in Italy* (vol. i., p. 22): "It might be advisable, when restorations are undertaken, to entrust them to skilful hands, and not to mere mechanical mosaists, ignorant of form and design, however able they may be in the technical difficulties of the art. Before touching monuments such as these, Italy should possess a school devoted to the study of the character and style of art in various periods. A competent person should be employed to study the mode in which emblems and accessories were used in different epochs. For there is no doubt that the period in which a monument was erected or adorned may be detected by the peculiar character of its emblems and accessories; and the use of false ones by restorers produces endless deception."

So also Paciaudus, in his *De Cultu S. Joannis Baptistæ*, who says:

"Was our Lord baptized by aspersion? This is so far from being so that nothing can be more contrary to truth, but it must be attributed to the error and ignorance of painters, who, being often unacquainted with history, or believing they could dare everything, sometimes greatly altered the subjects they portrayed." [63]

Certainly, pictorial representations, concerning whose testimony art-critics themselves are not agreed or whose archæological value is called in question, cannot be regarded as very important witnesses for a practice concerning which the literature of the period is so remarkably silent.

Art, however, is a most important and undoubted witness for immersion in this period. Of the representation of the baptism of Christ in the catacomb of San Ponziano outside of Rome, and which by Boldetti is assigned to the fifth or sixth century, Bottari, in his *Roma Sotterranea* (t. 1, p. 194), gives the following explanation:

"Upon the wall over the arch the Redeemer is represented up to his waist in the waters of the river Jordan, and upon his head rests the right hand of John the Baptist, who is standing upon the shore. It is by mistake that modern artists represent Christ in the Jordan up to his knees only, and John pouring water upon his head. And although on the portico of the church of San Lorenzo, outside of the walls of Rome, that saint is seen in a painting pouring water upon the head of San Romano, this was certainly not the case, as that picture is far more modern [it is of the twelfth century] than those of the first centuries, and the artist was evidently ignorant or wrongly informed concerning the acts of San Lorenzo. It is not improbable, however, that subsequently it became customary to pour water upon the head of the catechumen after he had been immersed.

"On the other shore an angel is seen upon a cloud, holding the Saviour's robe. The Holy Ghost descends like a dove and alights upon the Redeemer, and John places his hand upon the head of Christ to immerse him. A hart is also seen standing on the shore and looking fixedly at the water—symbol of the catechumen ardently desiring the waters of baptism, according as Jerome says in his *Commentary on the Forty-second Psalm:* 'He wishes to come to Christ, in whom is the source of light, that, being washed by baptism, he may receive the gift of the remission of sins.'"

In the ancient church of San Celso, at Milan, there is a church-book in which is a representation of the baptism of Christ, which Bugati, a canonical priest, in his *Memoir of St. Celsus,* assigns to the fifth or sixth century. Of this picture Bugati says:

"The Redeemer is represented immersed in the water, according to the ancient discipline of the church observed for many centuries in the administration of baptism. John holds in his left hand a curved and knotty staff, and places his right upon the Saviour's head. Finally, the Holy Spirit descends from heaven in the form of a dove. This scene is found depicted on the most ancient Christian monuments."

Still other witnesses for immersion during this period are the baptisteries, which, after the conversion of Constantine, when the rites of Christianity could be celebrated in public, were constituted for the administration of baptism. They are mentioned by Cyril of Jerusalem, Ambrose, and Augustine. They were generally spacious buildings, circular or octagonal in form, and containing a large font, or what is now called a baptistery. Such a building was necessary, in order to accommodate the multitudes who received baptism at the two great church festivals, Easter and Pentecost, to which the administration of the ordinance was for the most part restricted. These baptisteries, or baptismal churches, were commonly called *photisteria,* illuminatories. The baptistery of Santa Sophia, at Constantinople, was called "the great illuminatory." In the baptistery at Antioch three thousand were once gathered for baptism.

THE ACT OF BAPTISM. 89

The baptistery at Ravenna, which belongs to the fourth or fifth century, has a font ten feet in diameter and three and a half feet in depth. The so-called baptistery of Constantine, not far from the church of St. John of Lateran, in Rome, belongs to the fifth century, and is now known as San Giovanni in Fonte. It contains a circular marble basin about twenty-five feet in diameter and three feet deep, and was supplied with water from the Claudian aqueduct.

There are now in Italy nearly forty baptisteries which were erected in the fourth, fifth, sixth, or seventh century. Their general features we have already given.

In the fourth century, and probably earlier, baptism was administered after dark, and the service was made impressive in some places by the use of artificial light. "It would be difficult," says a writer in Smith's *Dictionary of Christian Antiquities* (Eng. ed., vol. i., p. 157), "to imagine any scene more moving than that pictured to us in the pages of St. Cyril, when, on the eve of the Saviour's resurrection and at the doors of the church of the 'Anastasis,' the white-robed band of the newly-baptized was seen approaching from the neighboring baptistery, and the darkness was turned into day in the brightness of unnumbered lights; and as the joyous shout swelled upward, 'Blessed is he whose unrighteousness is forgiven and whose sin is covered,' it might well be thought that angels' voices were heard echoing the glad acclaim, 'Blessed is the man unto whom the Lord imputeth no sin, and in whose spirit there is no guile.'" Gregory **Nazianzen** (*Orat. 40*) has a like thought: "The station thou shalt take before the great bema, after thy baptism, is a great foreshadowing of the glory that shall be from heaven; the psalmody wherewith thou shalt be received is a prelude of the hymns that thence shall sound; the lamps that thou shalt kindle set forth in mystery that procession of many lights wherewith bright and virgin souls shall go forth to meet their Lord, having the lamps of faith bright and burning."

CHAPTER IV.

FROM THE COUNCIL OF TOLEDO TO THE COUNCIL OF RAVENNA.

A. D. 633–1311.

THE decision of the Council of Toledo in favor of single immersion did not obtain wider recognition in the seventh century. Theodore, who was made archbishop of Canterbury in 669, and entrusted by Pope Vitalianus with the mission to England, enjoined in his *Penitential* trine immersion in the words of Apostolical Canon 50 :

"If any bishop or presbyter does not perform the one initiation with three immersions, but with giving one immersion only, into the death of the Lord, let him be deposed. For the Lord said not, ' Baptize into my death,' but ' Go, make disciples of all nations, baptizing them in the name of the Father, and of the Son, and of the Holy Spirit.'"

James of Edessa, who was prelate of Syria from 684 to 707, prepared a liturgy for use at baptismal services, in which occurred the following:

"The priest stands by the font and invokes the

Spirit, who descends from on high, and rests on the waters and sanctifies them, and makes new sons to God.

"When the child is plunged into the water, the priest says:

"'N. is baptized for sanctity and salvation and a blameless life and a blessed resurrection from the dead, in the name of the Father. Amen. And of the Son. Amen. And of the living and Holy Spirit, for life everlasting. Amen.'

"The deacons sing:

"'Descend, our brother, marked with the cross, and put on our Lord, and be mingled with his race, for it is a mighty race, as is said in his parable.'

"And when the child comes out of the water, they sing:

"'Expand thy wings, holy church, and receive the simple lamb which the Holy Spirit has begotten from the waters of baptism.

"'Of this baptism prophesied the son of Zacharias. "I," said he, "baptize with water, but he which is to come, with the Holy Spirit."

"'The heavenly army surround the baptistery, that from its waters they may receive sons like to God.

"'From the waters Gideon chose him men

that they might go forth to battle. From the waters of baptism Christ hath chosen worshippers to himself.'"

The Venerable Bede (673-735), in the following passage from his *Hom. in. Dom.* (1, post. Epiph.), makes an incidental allusion to the act of baptism as practised in his own time:

"The person to be baptized is seen to descend into the font; he is seen when he is dipped in the waters; he is seen to ascend from the waters; but what effect the washing of regeneration works in him can be least seen. Thus, the piety of the faithful alone knows that the candidate descends into the font a sinner, but ascends purified from guilt; he descends a son of death, but ascends a son of the resurrection; he descends a son of apostasy, he ascends a son of reconciliation; he descends a son of wrath, he ascends a son of mercy; he descends a son of the devil, he ascends a son of God." [64]

Germanus, Patriarch of Constantinople, who died in 740, says in his *Rerum Eccl. Contemplatio, Patrolog. Græc.* (tom. 98, p. 385, Migne, Paris, 1860):

"We have been baptized with reference to the death and resurrection of Christ himself. For by the descent into the water and the ascent, and by the three submersions, we symbolize and confess the three days' burial and the resurrection of Christ himself. And still further, also, because he was baptized in the Jordan by John," etc.[65]

In 754, while he was in France, Pope Stephen II. was asked by the monks of Cressy to decide upon the lawfulness of "baptizing an infant (in case of necessity occasioned by sickness) by pouring water on its head from a cup or the hands." He answered:

"This baptism, if administered in the name of the holy Trinity, holds good, especially when necessity requires that he who was detained by sickness, regenerated in this manner, should be made a participant of the kingdom of God."[66]

John of Damascus, who was born about A. D. 700, and who died not earlier than A. D. 756, says in his work *De Fide Orth.* (lib. iv., c. 9):

"Baptism exhibits Christ's death. Therefore buried with the Lord by baptism, as says the holy apostle."[67]

Also, in the same work, a little farther on:

"The rite of baptism is a type of Christ's death; for by the three immersions baptism portrays the three days of the Lord's burial."[68]

Also, in his *Parallels* (lib. iii., tit. 4), treating of baptism, he says:

"Israel, if he had not passed through the sea, would not have been delivered from Pharaoh; and thou, if thou pass not through the water, wilt not be delivered from the bitter tyranny of the devil."[69]

In Ep. 81, Ed. Quercet, Alcuin (735-804), the most learned Englishman of his time, the friend and counsellor of Charlemagne, wrote to Paulinus concerning the practice of single immersion in Spain. He said:

"From the midst of the thorns of the rural districts of Spain, and from the lurking-places of his envenomed perfidy, the old serpent now once more attempts to lift his head, which had been bruised, not by the club of Hercules, but by the power of the gospel, and in the cups of his ancient malice to mingle a new and accursed poison; and like a very freezing blast from the north, he has assaulted one side of the solid bulwarks of the church in his endeavor to change the rule of the holy baptism of Catholic custom, and by introducing the notion that it ought to be administered by invocation of the holy Trinity, indeed, but with a single immersion."

In Epistle 90 he says:

"The pagan becomes one of the catechumens. He renounces Satan and all his hurtful pomps, etc., and in the name of the holy Trinity he is baptized by trine immersion." [70]

In Epistle 113 he says:

"There are some who assert that there ought to be but one immersion, and who neglect to imitate in baptism the three days' burial of our Saviour, even when an apostle says, 'You have been buried with Christ in baptism.' Rom. vi. 4; Col. ii. 12. But there are others who are willing to use the trine immersion, but to invoke the whole Trinity at every immersion; thus they study to name all the three persons thrice; but the truth itself teaches, 'Go ye, therefore, and teach all nations, baptizing them in the name of the Father, and of the Son, and of the Holy Spirit.' Matt. xxviii. 19. What need of thrice repeating the whole Trinity if once suffices?" [71]

In his work *De Div. Offic.*, c. 19, he says:

"Then the priest baptizes the infant by trine immersion, invoking the holy Trinity only once, and speaking thus: 'I baptize you in the name of the Father,' and he immerses him once; 'and of the Son,' and he immerses him again; 'and of the Holy Spirit,' and he immerses him a third time." [72]

The *Ordo Romanus*, which was prepared in the eighth century, prescribed immersion:

THE ACT OF BAPTISM.

"'I immerse thee in the name of the Father,' and immerse once; 'and of the Son,' and immerse again; 'and of the Holy Spirit,' and immerse a third time."[73]

In 787 the Council of Calcuith, in England, by enactment, appointed the festivals of Easter and Whitsuntide for the administration of baptism, as in the Roman Church. In a report which they forwarded to Pope Adrian I., the legates Gregory and Theophylact refer to this fact in their account of the proceedings of the council, and in their communication make the following recommendation:

"That baptism be practised according to the canonical statutes, and not at any other time, except in great necessity; and that all in general know the Creed and the Lord's Prayer; and that all who take the children out of the font, and answer for those who cannot speak, know that they are sureties to the Lord, according to their sponsion, for the renouncing of Satan, his works and pomps, and for their believing of the Creed, that they may teach them the Lord's Prayer aforesaid and the Creed while they are coming to ripeness of age; for if they do not, what is promised to God in behalf of those who cannot speak, shall be with rigor exacted of them. Therefore we enjoin that this be charged on the memories of all people in general."⁷⁴

In his work *De Ordine Baptismi*, Theodulphus, who became Bishop of Orleans in 794 and died in 821, says:

"We die to sin when we renounce the devil and all his works; we are buried with Christ when we descend into the font of washing as into a sepulchre, and are immersed three times in the name of the holy Trinity; we rise with Christ when, purified of all our sins, we come out of the font as from a tomb."⁷⁵

Archbishop Magnus of Sens, who was consecrated at Rome by Leo III. in 801, prepared a work on *Baptism* by order of Charlemagne, in which he says:

"*Baptism* in Greek is translated *immersion* in Latin, ... and therefore the infant is immersed three times in the sacred font, that trine immersion may mystically show forth the three days' burial of Christ, and that the lifting up from the waters may be a likeness of Christ rising from the tomb."⁷⁶

Leidradus, Bishop of Lyons in 816, in a tract on *Baptism*, says:

"But we immerse three times that we may show forth the mystery of the three days' burial;

that whilst the infant is drawn out of the water three times, the resurrection of three days may be shown forth. . . . In the baptism of infants there ought to be no censure for immersing once or thrice, since in three immersions the trinity of Persons can be exhibited, and in a single immersion the oneness of Jehovah."[77]

In the sixth canon of the Council of Celichyth,—or Ceale-hythe, in the kingdom of Mercia,—held in 816, and at which Wulfred, Archbishop of Canterbury, presided, immersion was insisted upon in these words:

"And let the presbyters know that when they administer holy baptism they may not pour water upon the heads of the infants, but the infants must always be immersed in water, for the Son of God furnished an example in his own person for every believer when he was thrice dipped in the waves of the Jordan. In this manner it ought to be observed."[78]

Rabanus Maurus, who was made Archbishop of Mentz in 847, says in his *De Clericorum Institutione*, lib. i., c. 25:

"*Baptism*, in Greek *baptisma*, is translated into Latin by *tinctio*. And it is called immersion, not only because man is immersed in water, but because by the Spirit of grace he is changed for the better, and made far another being than he was before."[79]

So also in l. i., c. 28, he says:

"This trine immersion may represent the three days' burial of the Lord, as when the apostle says, 'So many of us as were baptized into Jesus Christ were baptized into his death.'"[80]

In his *De Sacr. Ordin.*, c. 14, he says, referring to baptism:

"After these things the fountain is consecrated and the candidate draws near to baptism itself, and thus in the name of the holy Trinity he is baptized by trine immersion. . . . Baptism ought therefore to be conferred by trine immersion, with the invocation of the holy Trinity."[81]

Walafrid Strabo, Abbot of Richenau, in his *De Offic. Eccles.*, c. 26, written about A. D. 840, referring to the practice of single immersion in Spain, says:

"Which single immersion—although at that time pleasing to the Spaniards, who asserted that trine immersion should be disused because certain heretics, for the purpose of denying the consubstantiality, had dared to propound the dogma that there are dissimilar substances in the Trinity, notwithstanding the more ancient use and the reason above stated—prevailed. For if we are to desert everything which heretics have perverted, nothing will be left us, since they have erred concerning even God himself, and they have twisted everything which seems to pertain to his worship, and have applied it as though it were peculiarly designed for the support of their errors. But why should I speak further? Suffice it to say that the trine immersion prevails everywhere in the world this day, and that it can by no means be changed, unless in accordance with a rash desire of novelty and to the scandal of the weak."[82]

Hincmar, who was made Archbishop of Rheims in 845 and died in 882, in an address to his presbyters on baptism, says:

"He is baptized by trine immersion in the name of the Father, and of the Son, and of the Holy Spirit, that just as the inner man, which is made after the image of the holy Trinity, through invocation of the holy Trinity, is restored to the same image, and as that which fell under subjection to death by three grades of transgression, being thrice raised out of the font, rises by grace to life; and as the inner man in the faith of the holy Trinity is to be created anew after the image of its Creator, so also the exterior man ought to be washed by trine immersion. So that what the

Spirit works invisibly in the soul, this the priest should imitate visibly in the water. For the original transgression was committed by three circumstances—by delight, by consent, and by the act; and so every sin is effected either by thought, word, or deed. Wherefore the trine ablution seems to answer to the three classes of sins. Or, if you choose, it should be used on account of original sin, which in infants avails to their destruction, or on account of those sins which in the case of men of more advanced age are added by the will, word, or deed. And because, according to the Holy Scriptures, there is one God, one faith, and one baptism, the candidate for baptism is thrice immersed in the name of the Father, and of the Son, and of the Holy Spirit, that the Trinity may appear to be one sacrament; and he is not baptized in the name of Father, Son, and Holy Spirit, but in one name, which is God, according to an apostle. Therefore, one God, one faith, one baptism."[83]

Canon 5 of the Council of Worms, A. D. 868, is almost word for word like the fifth canon of the fourth Council of Toledo, and favors single immersion. The reason for the enactment of the canons was the same in both cases:

"While some priests baptized with three immer-

THE ACT OF BAPTISM. 103

sions, and the others with but one, a schism was raised, endangering the unity of the church."[84]

This is the language of the Council of Toledo.

The Council of Tribur, A. D. 895, in a reference to trine immersion, made use of nearly the same words as Pope Leo I.:

"Trine immersion is an imitation of the three days' burial, and the rising again out of the water is an image of Christ rising from the grave."[85]

One of the oldest illustrated rituals of baptism, in a manuscript of the ninth century, is to be found in the library of La Minerva, at Rome, and one of the miniatures it contains is the oldest representation of the baptism of infants that has been found. The ritual prescribes immersion:

"And he baptizes with trine immersion, saying, 'I baptize thee in the name of the Father,' and immerses once; 'and of the Son,' and immerses again; 'and of the Holy Spirit,' and immerses a third time."[86]

The pictorial representation is in agreement with the ritual.

Atto, Bishop of Vercelli, who died in 960, has this remark in an exposition of Rom. vi. 4:

"We are baptized into his death, since as he died, so also we, when we renounce the devil and his works, the world and its pomp, in like manner die when we are immersed in water. And because he had said his death represents our death, and that he might show that his burial represents our burial, he added: 'Therefore we are buried with him by baptism into death.'"[87]

Fulbertus, who was made Bishop of Chartres in 1007 and died 1029, in a comment on Rom. vi. 4, says:

"We know, and know truly, that we were polluted by our first birth and purified by our second; therefore we are buried, and we die with Jesus Christ that we may be born again and quickened with him. The water and the Holy Spirit are united in that sacrament; the water denotes the burial, the Holy Spirit the life eternal. As, therefore, we have been informed that the body of our Lord Jesus Christ was buried in an earthly grave three days and three nights, so also a man immersed three times under an element allied to the earth is covered; and thus, whilst he is immersed in imitation of a vital mystery, he is buried; when he is raised he is awakened."[88]

Lanfranc, an Italian, who was born in 1005, and was made Archbishop of Canterbury by William the Conqueror in 1070 and died in 1089, achieved distinction as an author by his *Exposition of the Epistles of Paul*. In his note on Phil. iii. 10,

THE ACT OF BAPTISM. 105

"Being made conformable unto his death," he says:

"In baptism, for as Christ lay for three days in the sepulchre, so let there be a trine immersion when the act is administered."[89]

Theophylact, who was Bishop of Achrida about 1070, in his *Commentary on Nahum* (c. 1), says:

"For one baptism is spoken of, as also one faith, because of the doctrine respecting the initiation, being one in all the church, which has been taught to baptize with invocation of the Trinity, and to symbolize the Lord's death and resurrection by the threefold sinking down and coming up."[90]

So, also, in his note on the words in Acts i. 5, "Ye shall be baptized in the Holy Spirit," he says:

"The word *be baptized* signifies the abundance and, as it were, the riches of the participation of the Holy Spirit; as, also, in that perceived by the senses, he in a manner has who is baptized in water, bathing the whole body, while he who simply receives water is not wholly wetted in all places."[91]

In his note on 1 Cor. ix. 2, in which the apostle speaks of those who were "baptized unto Moses in the cloud and in the sea," he says:

"That is, they shared with Moses both the

shadow beneath the cloud and the passage through the sea; for seeing him first pass through, they also themselves braved the waters. As, also, in our case, Christ having first died and risen, we also are ourselves baptized, imitating death by the sinking down, and resurrection by the coming up. 'They were baptized unto Moses,' therefore, instead of 'They had him as a founder of the type of baptism;' for the being under the cloud and the passing through the sea were a type of baptism."[92]

The Use of Salisbury, a ritual ascribed to Osmond, who accompanied William the Conqueror to England in 1066, and was made Bishop of Salisbury in 1078, and which for a long period was generally followed in the churches in England, Wales, and Ireland, says:

"Then let the priest take the child by its sides in his hands; and having asked its name, let him baptize it by trine immersion, invoking the holy Trinity thus: 'N. I baptize in the name of the Father,' and let him immerse it once with its face toward the north and its head toward the east; 'and of the Son,' and let him immerse it again with its face toward the south; 'and of the Holy Spirit, Amen,' and let him immerse it a third time with its face toward the water."[93]

THE ACT OF BAPTISM. 107

It should be added, however, that in cases of necessity, but only in such cases, the *Use* allowed lay baptism by pouring or single immersion.

Gilbert, Bishop of Limerick, in Ireland, who lived in the early part of the twelfth century, in a work on the *Constitution of the Church* (*Patrol. Lat.*, vol. clix., p. 1000, Migne), says concerning the duty of a priest:

"It is his duty to administer baptism, to dip believers who have been exorcised, and who have confessed the holy Trinity, with three immersions in the sacred font." [94]

In the Romanesque church of St. Bartholomew at Liege is a bronze font made at Dinant by Lambert Patras in 1112. In Dr. W. N. Cote's *Archæology of Baptism* (pp. 255, 256) it is described as follows:

"It is cylindrical, resting on a base surrounded by twelve bulls, symbolizing, as appears by the inscription accompanying them, the twelve apostles. There is, doubtless, an allusion to the brazen sea in the court of Solomon's temple. On the outside are sculptured in very high relief, and in a very masterly style, the five following scenes: 1. John the Baptist preaching to the publicans and the soldiers, with the following inscription: *Facite ergo fructus dignos pœnitentiæ.* 2. John baptizing two Jews in the river Jordan: *Ego nos baptizo in aqua, venit autem fortior me post me.* 3. The baptism of Christ. The Saviour is represented of small size, half immersed in the Jordan, which rises in the centre of the composition like a small mountain; the Baptist stands on the left side, and the '*angeli ministrantes,*' as designated by the inscription, on the right. The eternal Father is represented above, looking down as if from a rainbow, and the Holy Ghost descends as a dove on the head of the Saviour: *Ego a te debeo baptizari et tu venis ad me.* 4. The baptism of Cornelius the centurion by Peter: *Cecidit Spiritus Sanctus super omnes qui audiebant verbum.* 5. The baptism of the philosopher Craton, at Ephesus, by John. On an open book in the hand of the evangelist is inscribed *Ego te baptizo in nomine Patris, et Filii, et Spiritus Sancti. Amen.*

"In the last two groups each of the figures is immersed to the breast in the circular font, and the blessing of God is represented by a hand issuing from a rainbow above, with the fingers extended, according to the Roman mode of benediction, and with a triple ray of light emanating from the outstretched hand."

Victor St. Hugo, a monk of the monastery of

THE ACT OF BAPTISM. 109

St. Victor, and one of the most celebrated men of his time, who died A. D. 1140, says in his *Summa Sentent.* (tract v., c. 3):

"This order of baptism is observed to show forth a double mystery; for ye were rightly immersed three times who have received baptism in the name of the Trinity, and ye were rightly immersed three times who have received baptism in the name of Jesus Christ, who arose from the dead on the third day; for this trine immersion is a figure of the Lord's burial, through which ye have been buried with Christ by baptism." [95]

Abelard (1079–1142), who in theological learning and dialectic skill, surpassed all of his contemporaries, says of baptism (*Patrol. Lat.*, Migne, vol. clxxviii., p. 1510):

"In baptism it is of no consequence whether you immerse the infant once or three times; by three immersions the Trinity can be exhibited, and by one the unity of the divinity." [96]

Pullus, an Englishman, a lecturer at Oxford, and afterward a professor of divinity in Paris, was created a cardinal in 1144. In a theological treatise (*Patrol. Lat.*, Migne, vol. cl., p. 315) he makes this reference to baptism:

"While the candidate for baptism is immersed, the death of Christ is suggested; while immersed, or covered with water, the burial of Christ is shown forth; while he is raised from the waters, the resurrection of Christ is proclaimed. The immersion is repeated three times out of reverence for the Trinity, and on account of the three days' burial of Christ. In the burial of the Lord the day follows the night three times; in baptism, also, trine emersion accompanies trine immersion."[97]

Bernard of Clairvaux (1091–1153) has this testimony in his sermon on the Lord's Supper:

"Baptism is the first of all the sacraments in which we are planted together with the likeness of his [Christ's] death. Hence trine immersion [*trina mersio*] represents the *triduum* [or three days] which we are about to celebrate."

Peter Lombard, who was made Bishop of Paris in 1159 and died about 1160, defines baptism (*Sentent. Quatuor*, lib. iv., dist. 3) thus:

"Baptism is called a dipping in—that is, a washing of the surface of the body."[98]

In the same connection he says:

"If the question is raised how many times immersion should be administered, we answer once or thrice, according to the various customs of the church."[99]

At the Council of Cashel, in 1172, which was called to secure uniformity in the English and

THE ACT OF BAPTISM. 111

Irish churches, and which was attended by two of the English clergy by order of Henry II., and also by all the archbishops and bishops of Ireland, it was decreed—

"That children shall be brought to the church, and shall there be baptized in pure water by trine immersion." [100]

Pope Alexander III. in 1175, in his *Extra. De Bapt.*, indicated the usual practice in the following words:

"If any one shall have immersed a boy thrice in water in the name of the Father, and of the Son, and of the Holy Spirit, Amen, and not have said, 'I baptize thee in the name of the Father,' the boy was not baptized." [101]

The following is from *Ordo Romanus X.*, an ordinal prepared in the latter part of the twelfth century, and describes the ordinance of baptism as administered at that time by the pope in the baptistery of the Lateran, in Rome. It is found in Father Mabillon's collection:

"The children—John, Peter, or Mary—being brought before him [the pontiff], he interrogates the person who presents them. What is your name? ANS. John. Then he goes on and says: John, dost thou believe in God, the Father almighty, the Creator of heaven and earth? ANS.

I do believe. Quest. Dost thou believe in Jesus Christ, his only Son, our Lord, who was born and suffered? Ans. I do believe. Quest. Dost thou believe in the Holy Ghost, the holy Catholic Church, the communion of saints, the remission of sins, the resurrection of the body, and life eternal? Ans. I do believe. Quest. John, wilt thou be baptized? Ans. I will. Then he baptizes him by trine immersion, mentioning the holy Trinity but once, as follows: 'I baptize thee in the name of the Father (and immerses him once), and of the Son (and immerses him again), and of the Holy Spirit (and immerses him a third time), that thou mayest have eternal life.'[102] Ans. Amen. The same to Peter and Mary. The three being baptized, the pope, with a mantle thrown over his surplice, goes to the place where is the chrism, whilst the younger of the chief deacons and the canon priests baptize the remaining children."

An order of baptism in a manuscript of the twelfth century, which formerly belonged to the church in Ravenna and is now in the library of the University of Bologna, resembles the Roman ordinal. The priest interrogates the candidate as to the Creed in three questions:

"Then taking him, he baptizes him with trine

THE ACT OF BAPTISM. 113

immersion [*sub trina mersione*], saying, Wilt thou be baptized? Ans. I will. Three times. And I baptize thee in the name of the Father, and immerses him once [*et mergit semel*], and of the Son, and immerses him again [*mergit iterum*], and of the Holy Spirit, and immerses him a third time [*mergit tertio*]; and taking him out of the font, the presbyter anoints him on the crown of the head in the form of a cross, saying, 'In the name of the Father +, and of the Son +, and of the Holy Spirit +. Amen.'"

In the third canon of the Westminster General Council, held in London in the year 1200, we find this rule:

"If a layman baptize a child in case of necessity, let all that follows after the immersion [the chrism, etc.] be performed by a priest."[103]

Similar is the twelfth of the *Constitutions* of Edmund in 1236:

"If a child be baptized by a layman, let what goes before the immersion and what follows after be fully supplied by a priest."[104]

The Council of Worcester, in 1240, enjoined trine immersion in these words:

"We enjoin that in every church where baptism is performed there shall be a font of stone of sufficient size and depth for the baptizing of children, and that it shall be decently covered. . . . And let the candidate for baptism always be thrice immersed." [105]

The council further decreed:

"But children baptized in case of necessity, if they recover, must be brought to the church, that those things which are wanting may be supplied—namely, those things which follow the immersion in baptism." [106]

Thomas Aquinas, "the Second Augustine," who died in 1274, says in his *Summa Theologiæ* (pars. 3, quest. 66, art. 7):

"The symbol of Christ's burial is more expressively represented by immersion, and for that reason this mode of baptizing is more common and more commendable." [107]

Sprinkling or pouring he thought might have been practised in the times of the apostles, as in the case of the three thousand baptized on the day of Pentecost; and he concludes the statement from which we have quoted above with the words:

"Although it is safer to baptize by immersion, because this is the more common use, baptism may be administered by sprinkling, or even by pouring." [108]

At the Council of Clermont, in 1268, it was decreed that if a layman had administered baptism in a case of necessity, the priest should ascertain in reference to the mode of administration; and if this were found to be satisfactory, only the parts of the ceremony that had been omitted should be supplied. The decree was as follows:

"At the font everything which is usually done shall be performed, the immersion only excepted. But if it is doubtful under what form of words the child has been baptized, then let the priest baptize him; but while he immerses him let him say, 'If thou art not already baptized, I baptize thee in the name of the Father, and of the Son, and of the Holy Spirit. Amen."[109]

Bonaventura, a distinguished theologian, who died in 1274, referring to the act of baptism (*Dist.*, 3, q. 1), says:

"The priest should hold the child by its sides; and having turned its face to the water, he should so immerse him as to have the head first turned to the east, second to the north, and third to the south."[110]

The fourth *Constitution*, adopted at Reading, England, in 1279, says:

"We think fit to explain what is provided in this present constitution concerning the reserving of children to be baptized till the general baptizing at Easter and Pentecost, out of our regard to that statute which seems to have been hitherto neglected — namely, that children born within eight days before Easter, and as many before Pentecost, be reserved to be baptized at those times, if it may be done without danger; so that they receive instruction between the time of their birth and their receiving perfect baptism, so that immersion alone remains to be performed on the day of baptism."[111]

The Council of Cologne, in 1280, put on record the following:

"We decree that baptism be celebrated in a worthy manner, with proper distinction of the words on the repetition of which the salvation of the baptized depends, and that he who baptizes, when he immerses the candidate in water, shall neither add to the words, nor take from them, nor change them, but shall say, 'Peter or John, I baptize thee in the name of the Father, and of the Son, and of the Holy Spirit. Amen.'"[112]

But when immersion, as in the case of an unborn child, was impossible, pouring was declared permissible; though if the infant survived, and there was doubt in reference to the baptism, conditional baptism was allowed.[113]

The Council of Nismes, in 1284, enacted the following decree:

"We admonish, therefore, that so soon as an infant is born, if it is in imminent danger of death, and if it cannot be brought to a presbyter, it shall be baptized by the males present in warm or in cold water, but not in any other liquid, and in a clean vessel of wood, stone, or some other material. But if a vessel cannot be had, let water be poured upon its head, and let the due form of words be used. . . . But let it be so done that the baptizer, while he thrice immerses the infant in water, shall say, 'Peter or Martin, I baptize thee in the name of the Father, and of the Son, and of the Holy Spirit. Amen.' Notwithstanding if but one immersion has been performed, the child will nevertheless be baptized. . . . But if a sufficient quantity of water cannot be had for wholly immersing the infant, let a certain quantity of water be poured upon the infant."[114]

The following is a decree of a council in the Netherlands in 1287:

"The administrator of baptism, in immersing the candidate in water, shall say these words, without addition, subtraction, or alteration, naming the child, 'Peter or John, I baptize thee in the name of the Father, and of the Son, and of the

Holy Spirit;' and to avoid all danger let the priest not immerse the head of the child in water, but let him hold the child discreetly with one hand, and let him three times pour water upon the crown of his head out of a basin or a clean and decent vase."[115]

The Council of Exeter, in the same year, made this requirement:

"At the time of birth let water be provided, in which, if it shall be necessary, the child may be immersed, saying, 'I baptize.' . . . Let the water in which the child was immersed be poured into the baptistery."[116]

The Council of Utrecht, in 1293, enacted the following:

"We appoint that the head be put three times in the water, unless the child be weak or sickly or the season cold; then water may be poured by the hand of the priest, lest by plunging or coldness or weakness the child should be injured and die."[117]

Guillaume Durant, Bishop of Mende, 1286–1296, gave the following directions to his clergy:

"Each basilica should be provided, if possible, with stone fonts. Otherwise, let there be a wooden basin made expressly for the purpose. . . . Teach frequently your people the form of baptism, in

THE ACT OF BAPTISM.

order that they may, in case of necessity, observe it scrupulously, to wit: that he who baptizes, after giving a name to the child, and made the sign of the cross upon the water, must plunge the infant three times in the form of the cross in warm or cold water, saying, 'P., or C., I baptize thee in the name of the Father, and of the Son, and of the Holy Spirit. Amen.' And if he cannot say the words in Latin, let him pronounce them in the common language. Should he have immersed the child but once, and forgotten to give it a name, and not used the word *ego*, I, if he has said the remaining part of the form, the child shall be considered as duly baptized."[118]

Pope Celestine, who died in 1296, says in his *Opusculum Octavum:*

"Baptism is the washing of the body [*corporis ablutio*], which represents the inner purification of the soul. How great, therefore, the virtue of water, since it can reach the body and at the same time cleanse the heart!"

At the Council of Ravenna, in 1311, it was made allowable to administer baptism either by sprinkling or immersion:

"Baptism is to be administered by trine aspersion or immersion [*sub trina aspersione, vel immersione*]."

REMARKS.

During this period, also, trine immersion held its place as the general rule. The decision of the Fourth Council of Toledo, which allowed single immersion, in opposition to the Arians in Spain, received no countenance in other parts of Christendom during the seventh and eighth centuries. In the ninth century, at the Council of Worms, the decision of the Fourth Council of Toledo was reaffirmed, but the decision had only a local recognition. It is worthy of notice, also, that the decision of the Council of Worms, like that of the Fourth Council of Toledo, was carried, in order to prevent a schism in the church. In the thirteenth century, the Council of Nismes, which prescribed trine immersion as the general rule, allowed single immersion in cases of necessity. No other councils during the period favor single immersion.

In 669, the Archbishop of Canterbury went so far as to reissue Apostolical Canon 50, which directed that a bishop or presbyter should be deposed who practised single immersion. In 816, Leidradus, who admits that trine immersion was the general rule, would censure no one for immersing once or thrice. Walafrid Strabo, in the same century, testifies to the general prevalence of trine immersion. "Trine immersion," he says, "prevails everywhere in the world this day." But this practice, which had so long held its place in the church, was evidently growing less and less general; so that the Council of Worcester, in 1240, found it necessary to enjoin trine immersion.

All of the baptismal offices of this period also bear witness to the general practice of trine immersion throughout Christendom.

The testimony of the baptisteries, of which a large number were erected during this period, is, like that of the preceding period, wholly in favor of immersion. We need refer to only one or two. In the baptistery at Parma, which was commenced in 1196, there is a large octagonal basin, eight feet in diameter and four feet deep. The inscription on the rim records the fact that the font was made by Johannes Pallassonus in 1299. There is evidence, which will be produced in its proper place, that immersion was practised in this font as late as the close of the sixteenth century.

The baptistery of Verona, called S. Giovanni in Fonte, was built by Bishop Bernardo in 1135 to take the place of an earlier one destroyed in 1116 by an earthquake. Dr. Cote (*Baptism and Baptisteries*, p. 146) describes it as follows: "In the centre is a large octangular basin of marble, twenty-eight feet in circumference, hewn out of a single block of Venetian marble. By actual measurement we found the depth of this font to be four feet and a half."

The first reference to pouring during this period we find in the *Ninety-Fifth Excerption of Eigbright*, in 740, by which, in cases of necessity—that is, in order "to snatch a soul from the devil"—baptism by pouring is regarded as valid baptism. There were those evidently who had grave doubts in reference to this innovation. In 754, Pope Stephen II. was asked by the monks of Cressy to decide the question that had been raised. It is to be noticed that in his declaration in favor of the validity of pouring he had in mind cases of supposed necessity.

The practice seems gradually to have increased, so that the Council of Celichyth, in 816, found it necessary to denounce pouring.

Thomas Aquinas, in the thirteenth century, seems to have been the first writer to justify sprinkling or pouring as sanctioned by the New Testament. He says that the baptism of the three thousand on the day of Pentecost suggests such a practice at that time. But he admits that in his day immersion was the more common use, and more worthy of praise.

That at the close of this period sprinkling or pouring came to be used in other cases than those of necessity, Höfling (*Das Sacrament der Taufe*, s. 51, 52) thinks is to be explained by the fact that at this time adult baptism had given place almost wholly to infant baptism. Dr. Philip Schaff, in his *History of the Apostolic Church* (p. 569, note), says: "Not till the end of the thirteenth century did sprinkling become the rule and immersion the exception—partly from the gradual decrease in the number of adult baptisms, partly from considerations of health and convenience, all children having now come to be treated as *infirmi*."

Brenner, a Roman Catholic writer, in his *Geschichtliche Darstellung der Verrichtung der Taufe*, in which he reviews the history of baptism from the first century to our own times, thus (on page 306) sums up the evidence which the first thirteen hundred years of the Christian era furnish: "Thirteen hundred years was baptism generally and regularly an immersion of the person under the water, and only in extraordinary cases a sprinkling or pouring with water; the latter, moreover, was disputed as a mode of baptism—nay, even forbidden." [119]

In reference to the Council of Ravenna, it should be noticed that now, for the first time in the history of the church, immersion and sprinkling were made indifferent by an act of legislation; also, that the council represented only a single province.

CHAPTER V.

FROM THE COUNCIL OF RAVENNA TO THE WESTMINSTER ASSEMBLY.

A. D. 1311–1644.

THOUGH the Council of Ravenna recognized trine aspersion and trine immersion as equally valid, the latter was only gradually superseded. Yet it is worthy of mention that the latest baptistery erected in Italy, that of Pistoja, which stands opposite the cathedral and is known as San Giovanni Rotondo, was built in 1337.

The Council of Prague, in 1355, made the following decree:

"Let the presbyters take heed lest any negligence be committed, either in the putting together or in the expression of the proper form of words, as well as in the immersion in water, with which the whole value of baptism is connected. As to the form, let the immersion be trine, in this manner—that at once, when the administrator begins to utter the prescribed form, he does that which is first, and that which is last when he finishes." [120]

THE ACT OF BAPTISM.

John Wickliffe, who died in 1384, in a sermon on the necessity of baptism in order to salvation, based on the words in John iii. 5, says: "The church has ordained that in case of necessity any baptized person may administer the ordinance;" and adds:

"Nor is it material whether they be dipped once or thrice, or water be poured on their heads; but it must be done according to the custom of the place where one dwells."[121]

In 1420, John Gerson, Chancellor of the University of Paris, in answer to the question, "How many times should one be immersed?" answered:

"According to the usage of the church, either once, to denote the unity of the divine essence, or three times, to represent the trinity of the Persons."[122]

Lyndwood, who was Dean of the Arches in 1422, and the author of a valuable work on the *English Constitutions* (*Provinciale*, lib. iii., tit. 24, 25), refers to the practice of dipping infants in baptizing them, and adds:

"But this is not to be accounted of the necessity of baptism, but it may be given also by pouring or sprinkling; and this holds especially where the custom of the church allows it."

At the Council of Florence, in 1439, there was a discussion (Harduin, *Conc.*, t. ix., p. 620) between Mark of Ephesus on the part of the Greeks, and Gregory the monk on the part of the Latins. Mark brought against the latter the charge that they had "two baptisms, one administered by trine immersion, and the other by pouring water upon the top of the head." Gregory replied:

"That there are two baptisms no one ever asserted, for holy baptism is one; . . . and that the trine immersion is necessary is evident, for thus has it been handed down by the saints to signify the three days' burial of the Lord. So, indeed, it has been handed down, and so the rituals of the Latins teach that it shall be observed."[123]

Yet he admits a mingling of immersion and pouring:

"But we by no means immerse the infants' heads, for we cannot teach them to hold the breath, nor can we prevent the water from going through their ears, nor can we close their mouths. But we so put them into the font as to omit nothing which is really necessary for the carrying out of the tradition. . . . And lest the head, in which is the seat of all the senses and the

THE ACT OF BAPTISM.

vehicle of the soul, may be without holy baptism, we take up water in the hollow of the hand out of the sacred font, and pour it over it, etc. For when a tyrant charged it upon Saint Apollonius as a reproach that he had not been washed in baptism, and that, therefore, he was not a Christian, God, in kindness, heard the saint's prayers and satisfied his desires, for a cloud, being sent down from above, bathed his head in dew. If, therefore, pouring upon the head be not baptism, it would not have been so done, but in some other way."

In the first lower-Saxon Bible, 1470–80, *baptizein* was translated by the word *doepen*, "to dip." John i. 33 read as follows:

"But he who sent me to dip in water."

Matt. iii. 11 read:

"And I, indeed, dip you in water."[124]

The Council of Padua, in 1470, made the following decree in reference to baptism:

"The custom hitherto introduced should be observed either by immersion or by pouring."[125]

In the Augsburg Bible, 1473–75, *baptizein* is rendered by the word *taufen*, "to dip." John i. 33 read:

"But he who sent me to dip in water."

Matt. iii. 11 read:

"And I, indeed, dip you in water."[126]

The first printed *Würzburg Liturgy*, which was published in 1482, contained these words:

"The priest, thrice immersing or thrice washing the infant with water, says," etc.[127]

The first *Bamberg Liturgy*, in 1491, had this injunction, prescribing pouring only:

"Baptize an infant under this form of words: 'And I baptize you in the name of the Father,' pouring, etc., 'and of the Son,' pouring, etc."[128]

John, Bishop of Regensburg, in 1512, gave the following direction:

"Let baptism be administered so that over the candidate pure water shall be poured with this form of words: 'N., I baptize,'" etc.[129]

In 1522, Erasmus published his *Colloquia*, written in England, in which he says:

"We dip children all over in cold water, in a stone font."

Luther's *Order of Baptism*, published in 1523, contains the following direction:

"Then let him take the child and dip it into the baptism."[130]

This agrees with what he says in his sermon on baptism:

"Although in many places it is no longer the custom to immerse the children entirely at baptism, but only to pour upon them with the hand, yet rightly, according to the formula, the child, or every one who is baptized, should be let down wholly into the water, and baptized and taken out. In this way will the requirements of the sign be fully met." [131]

So also in his work on the *Babylonian Captivity*, after speaking of the apostle Paul's representation of baptism as a symbol of death and resurrection, Luther says:

" On this account I could wish that such as are to be baptized should be completely immersed in water, according to the meaning of the word and the signification of the ordinance—not because I think it necessary, but because it would be beautiful to have a full and perfect sign of so perfect and full a thing, as also without doubt it was instituted by Christ." [132]

In his work on the *Sacrament of Baptism* he begins thus:

"First, *baptism* is a Greek word. In Latin it can be translated *immersion,* as when we plunge something into water that it may be completely covered with water; and although that custom has been given up by most persons—for they do not wholly submerge the children, but only pour on them a little water—yet they ought to be completely immersed and straightway drawn out." [133]

As to the practice of the Anabaptists, the first information we have is in the year 1525, when Rudolph Thomam was brought before the court at Zurich, in Switzerland, for trial. He testified that a few friends were invited to his house at Zollikon, near Zurich, and that others, whom he had not invited, came in one after another and filled the room. Then he described what was done at the meeting:

"After they had long read and conversed together, John Brubbach of Zurich arose and wept aloud, saying that he was a great sinner, and desiring the others to pray for him. Hereupon Blaurock asked him if he desired the grace of God. He replied, 'Yes.' Then Mantz rose and said, 'Who will forbid me to baptize this person?' 'No one,' replied Blaurock. He then took a dipper of water and baptized him in the name of the Father, the Son, and the Holy Spirit. Then Hottinger rose and desired baptism, and Mantz baptized him." [134]

Early the next morning Blaurock baptized Thomam and his son-in-law, and subsequently his whole family were baptized. Marx Bossart, the son-in-law, testified as follows:

THE ACT OF BAPTISM.   131

"That Mantz and Blaurock came to them, and after supper read in the Testament. Then John Brubbach rose, lamented his sins and wept, and desired the sign of conversion—namely, that he should be sprinkled in the name of the Father, the Son, and the Holy Spirit. Then Blaurock sprinkled him. Afterward he [Bossart] had desired the sign, and [the next morning] Blaurock sprinkled him also."[135]

In 1525, Blaurock, after his release from the prison in Zurich, went to Zollikon and baptized Henry Aberlin. "He took a handful of water and baptized him."[136] John Müller testified in court:

"He had a curiosity to see how they baptized, for Aberlin had told him that they put their hands into a vessel of water used for soaking leather, and with it sprinkled the persons baptized."[137]

In April, 1525, Hubmaier, it being Easter, the customary season for baptism, called his followers together, and having sent for a pail of water, "solemnly baptized three hundred persons at one time."[138]

About the same time Conrad Grebel, one of the leaders of the Swiss Anabaptists, immersed Wolfgang Ulimann of St. Gall in the Rhine at Schaffhausen. Kessler, in his *Sabbata* (vol. i., s. 266), says:

"Wolfgang Ulimann, on the way to Schaffhausen, met Conrad Grebel, who instructed him so highly in the knowledge of Anabaptism that he would not be sprinkled out of a dish, but was drawn under and covered over with the water of the Rhine by Grebel." [139]

Kessler adds that Grebel afterward visited St. Gall and baptized many in the Sitter River. Dr. Howard Osgood, professor in the Rochester Theological Seminary, in a communication to the *Religious Herald*, says: "I was at St. Gall in 1867, and made special investigation on this point. A mountain-stream sufficient for all sprinkling-purposes flows through the city, but in no place is it deep enough for the immersion of a person, while the Sitter River is between two and three miles away, and is gained by a difficult road. The only solution of this choice was that Grebel sought the river in order to immerse the candidates."

In his treatise, *Von dem christlichen Tauff der Gläubigen*, published in 1525, Balthaser Hubmaier, one of the most prominent of the Swiss Anabaptists, says:

"To baptize in water is to pour over the confessor of his sins external water, according to the divine command, and to inscribe him in the number of the separate upon his own confession and desire." [140]

In the *Strasburg Order of Baptism* (Protestant), published in 1525, we find the following:

"The minister, with the pouring out of the water, says, 'I baptize thee,'" etc.

In 1527, at Nicholsburg, in Moravia, Hubmaier published *A Form of Baptizing in Water those who are Instructed in Faith*. In this occurs the following:

"Do you desire upon this faith and duty to be baptized in water, according to the institution of Christ, and be thus incorporated and inscribed in the external Christian church for the remission of your sins? Then say, 'I desire it, God helping me.'"

The formula to be employed follows: "I baptize thee in the name of the Father, and the Son, and the Holy Spirit, for the pardon of thy sins. Amen." [141]

In the same year Zwingli published his *Elenchus contra Catabaptistas*. The word *Catabaptistas*, a word of post-classical Greek, means "one who dips or drowns." The decree of the Council of Zurich, in 1527, against the Anabaptists, in which occurred the words, "*Qui iterum mergat, mergatur,*" seems to indicate that at that time immersion had become the prevailing mode among the Anabaptists in Switzerland. Even in 1525, in his *Uiber doctor Balthazar's taufbüchlin*, Zwingli speaks of Hubmaier and his companions as "bath, (I should have said) Baptist, companions." [142]

In his *Vom Touf*, published in 1525, Zwingli refers to the general custom in his time as "pouring or dipping." [143] Sometimes he speaks of baptism *in* water, and sometimes of baptism *with* water. Referring to Rom. vi. 3, he says:

"Know ye not that he who is dipped into water (whereby he makes manifest his obedience to Christ) is dipped into the death of Christ? . . . Do ye not see that as we are thrust into the water, as if buried with Christ—that is, in his death—so we thereby signify that we also are dead to the world?" [144]

Johannes Landsberger, a Bavarian (sometimes called an Anabaptist, and certainly at one time an Anabaptist in his views), wrote a short treatise on baptism—at least, it is attributed to him—in which some objections to infant baptism are considered, and which was published in 1528. In it we find the following reference to the act of baptism:

"When one brings the child to baptism, and

in the pouring or sprinkling says, 'I baptize thee,'" etc.[145]

In 1528, William Tyndale published his *Obedience of a Christian Man*, in which (p. 143) he says:

"The plunging into the water signifieth that we die and are buried with Christ as concerning the old life of sin which is Adam. And the pulling out again signifieth that we rise again with Christ in a new life full of the Holy Ghost, which shall teach us and guide us, and work the will of God in us, as thou seest. Rom. vi."

In his *Doctrinal Treatises* (p. 277) there is a passage which shows the popular feeling in England in reference to the mode of baptism at the beginning of the Reformation:

"Behold how narrowly the people look on the ceremony! If aught be left out, or if the child be not altogether dipped in the water, or if, because the child is sick, the priest dare not plunge him into the water, but pour water on his head, how tremble they! how quake they! 'How say ye, Sir John?' [the priests were then called 'Sir'], say they; 'is this child christened enough? Hath it his full christendom?' They believe verily that the child is not christened."

J. Bugenhagen—often called Pomeranus, from

the name of his native district, and who was a friend and coadjutor of Luther at Wittenberg—in a book published in 1542, affirms:

"That he was desired to be a witness of a baptism in the year 1529; that when he had seen the minister only sprinkle the infant, wrapped in swaddling-clothes, on the top of the head, he was amazed, because he had neither heard nor seen any such thing, nor yet read in any history, except in the case of necessity, in bedridden persons. In a general assembly, therefore, of all the ministers of the word who were convened, he asked a certain minister, John Fritz by name, who was sometime minister of Lubeck, how the sacrament of baptism was administered at Lubeck. Who for his piety and candor did answer gravely that the infants were baptized naked at Lubeck, after the same fashion altogether as in Germany. But from whence and how that peculiar manner of baptizing had crept into Hamburg he was ignorant."

Meurer, in his *Life of Bugenhagen* (p. 48), states the case a little more fully. He says:

"Once when Bugenhagen stood godfather to a child in Hamburg, the administrator took the infant just as it was in its swaddling-clothes, and baptized it only on the top of its head. Bugenhagen was confounded, for he had neither u nor heard nor read in any history of such a th. before, except in cases of necessity. So he called all the pastors and chief preachers together, and they told him that this was an old custom in Hamburg. Mr. John Fritz, however, who had been settled at Lubeck, said that at Lubeck children were baptized, as they were everywhere in Germany, naked, and how it happened that there was such a difference here he didn't know. It was decided to keep the matter quiet for the present; and he did not attack the abuse seriously at once, lest the people should get the idea that those children which had been baptized in this improper way, and yet with the best intentions on their part, had not received the true baptism of Christ. Meanwhile, they appealed to Luther, and received as answer that their practice was surely an abuse that should be abolished, but care should be taken to avoid a public scandal on the subject. Hereupon Bugenhagen laid down in the twenty-eighth article of the Hamburg *Church Discipline* that, cases of necessity excepted, baptism should be performed either by complete immersion, or, according to the custom in almost all Germany, in Lubeck and elsewhere, as well as in the ancient church, by pouring a handful of water three times over the head and back of the naked child."

The *Manuale ad usum Sarum* [Salisbury], printed in 1530, made the following requirement for public baptism:

"Then let the priest take the child, and having asked his name baptize him by dipping him in the water thrice," etc.

John Frith, a companion of William Tyndale, and mentioned by Bugenhagen above, in a *Treatise on Baptism*, written in 1533 (he was burned at Smithfield, July 4, 1533), says:

"The signe in baptisme is the plounging downe in the material water, and liftynge up agayne, by the whiche, as by an outward badge, we are knowen to be of the number of them whiche professe Christ to be theyr Redeemer and Saviour."

In the *Order of Baptism* adopted by the Reformed church in Zurich, Switzerland, in the edition of 1535, occurs the following:

"Then the minister takes the child upon his hand over the font, and says to the sponsors, 'Is it your desire now that this child shall be baptized in the baptism of our Lord Jesus Christ? If so, say "Yes," and name the child.' The sponsors reply 'Yes,' and name the child. Thereupon the minister thrice pours water upon the child and says, 'N., I baptize thee,'" etc.[146]

The first Helvetic Confession, which was drawn up at Basel in 1536, at a conference of which Bucer, Capito, Bullinger, Myconius, Leo Juda, and others were members, has the following article concerning baptism:

"Baptism, by an institution of the Lord, is a bath of regeneration, which the Lord offers to his elect for a visible sign through the ministry of the church, as is explained above. In this bath we baptize our children," etc.[147]

James Sadolet, secretary to Pope Leo X., and made a cardinal by Pope Paul III. in 1536, says in his *Commentary on Paul's Epistle to the Romans* (ch. vi., vs. 4–8):

"Our trine immersion in water at baptism, and our trine emersion, denote that we are buried with Christ in the faith of the true Trinity, and that we rise again with Christ in the same belief."[148]

The Lower House of Convocation in England, in 1536, sent to the Upper House a protest against certain "profane sayings" current among the people, and asked the concurrence of the Upper House in condemning them. Among these sayings was the following:

"17. That it is as lawful to christen a child in

a tub of water at home, or in a ditch by the way, as in a font-stone in the church."

Menno, in his *Fundamental Book on the Saving Doctrine of Christ*, published in 1539, makes this reference to baptism as practised in his time:

"Paul calls baptism a water-bath of regeneration. Tit. iii. 5. Ah, dear Lord! how sorely thy word has been misinterpreted! Is it not a pity upon pity that with this clear passage they should defend their set-up idolatrous infant baptism, and pretend that in baptism the children are born again—that right or second birth is merely a thrusting into the water?"[149]

It has been supposed that in a passage in his *Explanation of Christian Baptism* (*Werken*, p. 409) Menno expressed his own view of the act of baptism, and his words have been translated by Morgan Edwards and others as follows: "After we have searched ever so diligently, we shall find no other baptism besides dipping in water which is acceptable to God and maintained in his word." But the passage is not thus correctly rendered. What Menno has in view is the representation that Christ and the apostles taught two kinds of baptism—that of believers and infants; and he says: "However diligently we seek, night and day, yet we find no more than one baptism in water that is pleasing to God expressed and contained in God's word—namely, this baptism on faith."[150]

Prof. Howard Osgood, of Rochester Theological Seminary, says that in all of Menno's writings he has found only two passages which seem to indicate the mode of baptism practised by Menno. On page 22 of the folio edition, 1681, he says: "I think that these [to love enemies, crucify flesh and lust] and similar commands are more painful and difficult to perverse flesh, which is naturally so prone to follow its own way, than to receive a handful of water." On page 88 of the same edition Menno says: "How any one who is so unbelieving and rebellious that he refuses God a handful of water can conform himself to love his enemies, to mortify the flesh to the service of his neighbor, and to take up the cross of Christ, I will leave the serious reader to reflect upon in the fear of God."

The Council of Trent, 1545–1563, authorized a catechism, which has this direction concerning baptism (*Catech.*, pt. ii., ch. 2, quest. 17, 18):

"Pastors . . . must briefly explain that by the common custom and practice of the church there are three ways of administering baptism. For those who ought to be initiated with this sacrament are either immersed into the water, or have the water poured upon them, or are sprinkled with the water. And whichsoever of these rites be observed, we must believe that baptism is rightly administered; for in baptism water is used to signify the spiritual ablution which it accomplishes. Hence, baptism is called by the apostle *a laver* (Tit. iii. 5; Eph. v. 26); but ablution is not more really accomplished by the immersion of any one in water, which was long observed from the earliest times of the church, than by the effusion thereof, which we now perceive to be the general practice, or aspersion, the manner in which there is reason to believe Peter administered baptism when on one day he converted and baptized three thousand persons. Acts ii. 41. But whether the ablution be performed once or thrice must be held to make no difference; for that baptism was formerly, and may still be, validly administered in the church in either way is sufficiently evident from the epistle of Gregory the Great to Leander. The rite, however, which each individual finds observed in his own church is to be retained by the faithful."

In 1545, Calvin published a *Form of Administering the Sacraments*, which in 1536 he had drawn up for the use of his church in Geneva. In this occurs the following:

"Then the minister of baptism pours water on the infant, saying, 'I baptize thee,'" etc.

In his celebrated *Institutes* (lib. iv., cap. 15, sec. 19), he says:

"Whether the baptized person is wholly immersed, and that three times or once, or whether water is only poured or sprinkled upon him, is of no consequence. In that matter churches ought to be free according to the different countries. The very word *baptize*, however, signifies *to immerse*, and it is certain that immersion was observed by the ancient church."[151]

So, also, in his *Commentary on Acts* (viii. 38), he says:

"'They descended into the water.' Here we perceive what was the rite of baptizing among the ancients, for they immersed the whole body; now the custom has become established that the minister only sprinkles the body or the head."

In the year 1545 (2d ed. 1567) the Anabaptists in Moravia published a *Confession of Faith*, which was drawn up by Peter Riedermann, who died Dec. 1, 1556, in Pruzga, Hungary. In the section in which the administration of baptism is referred to (*Mittheilungen aus dem Antiquariate,* von S. Calvary, & Co., Band 1, s. 309) **Riedermann** says:

"Then the baptizer commands the candidate to humble himself with bended knees before God and his church, and takes pure water and pours it upon him, and says, 'I baptize thee in the name of the Father, Son, and Holy Spirit.'"[152]

Cranmer's *Catechism* of 1548, which Schaff (*Creeds of Christendom*, vol. i., p. 655) says "was for the most part a translation of the Latin catechism of Justus Jonas," has this testimony concerning the act of baptism:

"Baptisme and the dippyng into the water doth betoken that the olde Adam, with al his synne and evel lustes, ought to be drowned and kylled by daily contrition and repentance, and that, by renewynge of the Holy Gost, we ought to rise with Christ from the death of synne and to walke in a new lyfe, that our new man maye lyve everlastyngly in righteousness and truthe before God, as Saincte Paule teacheth, saying, 'Al we that are baptized in Christe Jesu are baptized in hys death. For we are buried with him by baptisme into deth,'" etc.

In *The Book of the Common Prayer and Administration of the Sacraments and Ceremonies of the Church, after the Use of the Church of England,*

THE ACT OF BAPTISM. 145

printed in London in 1549, trine immersion is enjoined in these words:

"Then the priest shall take the child in his hands and ask the name, and naming the child shall dip it in the water thrice, first dipping the right side; second, the left side; the third time dipping the face toward the font; so it be discreetly and warily done, saying,

"'N., I baptize thee in the name of the Father, and of the Son, and of the Holy Ghost. Amen.'

"And if the child be weak, it shall suffice to pour water upon it, saying the aforesaid words."

The *Agenda* of the church of Mentz, published in 1551, has the following:

"Then let the priest take the child in his left arm; and holding him over the font, let him with his right hand, three several times, take water out of the font and pour it on the child's head, so that the water may wet its head and shoulders."

In a note it is added that immersion, single or trine, may be used, but a preference is expressed for pouring, on account of the possible infirmity either of the child or of the priest, thus:

"That therefore there may not be one way for the sick and another for the healthy, one for children and another for bigger persons, it is better that the minister of this sacrament do keep the safest way, which is to pour water thrice, unless the custom be to the contrary."[153]

In the same year, at Wittenberg, the Saxon Confession of Faith was adopted by the superintendents, pastors, and professors, that it might be presented to the Council of Trent. This Confession was published by Melanchthon, and contains the following in reference to baptism:

"Baptism is an entire action—to wit, a dipping and a pronouncing of these words, 'I baptize thee,—that is, I testify by this immersion that thou art washed from sin," etc.[154]

The Book of Common Prayer, published in London, in 1552, contains the following direction:

"Then the priest shall take the child in his hands and ask the name, and naming the child shall dip it in the water, so it be discreetly and warily done, saying,

"'N., I baptize thee in the name of the Father, and of the Son, and of the Holy Ghost. Amen.'

"And if the child be weak, it shall suffice to pour water upon it, saying the foresaid words."

In the Würtemburg ritual of 1553 occurs the following:

"Then let the minister sprinkle the child with water, disrobed, and say with clear, loud, and distinct voice, 'N., I baptize thee,'" etc.[155]

The liturgy of the church of the foreign residents at Frankfort, published in 1555, had this requirement:

"Then let the minister, before whom, on a table, is placed pure water in a basin, baptize the child, throwing the water by the hand upon his head, with these words: 'N., I baptize thee,'" etc.[156]

The Baden ritual of 1556 is as follows:

"Then let the minister, with the hand nearly full of water, thrice sprinkle the child, and say with a clear, loud, and distinct voice, 'N., I baptize thee,'" etc.[157]

In *The Form of Prayer and Administration of the Sacraments, Used in the English Church at Geneva, and Published in* 1556, *Approved by the Famous and Godly Learned Man John Calvin*, occurs the following:

"'N., I baptize thee in the name of the Father, and of the Sonne, and of the Holy Ghoste.' And as he speaketh these words he taketh water in his hand, and layeth it upon the childe's forehead; which done, he giveth thanks, as followeth."

Watson, Bishop of Lincoln, in 1558, published a volume of sermons on the *Seven Sacraments*. In the fourth of these he says:

"Though the ancient tradition of the church has been, from the beginning, to dip the child three times, etc., yet that is not of such necessity but that, if it be but once dipped in the water, it is sufficient. Yea, and in a time of great peril and necessity, if the water be but poured on the head, it will suffice."

The Liturgy of Zurich, 1559, set aside immersion and required sprinkling:

"Thereupon the minister sprinkles (not immerses) the child thrice with water, saying."[158]

The Espach ritual of 1560 has the following direction:

"Then shall the pastor take the child, disrobed, and pour water upon its head, giving its name, and saying, 'N., I baptize thee,'" etc.[159]

The Belgic Confession of 1561, in Article 34, which treats of "Holy Baptism," says:

"Therefore he has commanded all those who are his to be baptized with pure water, in the name of the Father, and of the Son, and of the Holy Ghost; thereby signifying to us that as water washeth away the filth of the body when poured upon it, and is seen on the body of the baptized when sprinkled upon him, so doth the blood of Christ, by the power of the Holy Ghost, internally sprinkle the soul, cleanse it from its sins, and regenerate us from children of wrath unto children of God. . . . Neither doth this baptism only avail us at the time when the water is poured upon us and received by us, but also through the whole course of our life."[160]

The ritual of the Elector Frederic of the Palatinate, 1563, says:

"Let then the minister request that they give the child's name, and afterward sprinkle it with water and say, 'N., I baptize thee,'" etc.[161]

The second Würzburg *Agenda*, 1564, says:

"The priest, taking water from the font with his right hand, pours it over the child three times."[162]

The second Helvetic Confession, 1566, in Chapter 20, "Concerning Baptism," says:

"And so we are baptized—that is, we are washed or sprinkled with visible water."[163]

In the Pomeranian ritual, 1569, occurs the following:

"Let him take the child and sprinkle it thrice with water, and say, 'And I baptize thee,'" etc.[164]

In the Austrian *Agenda* of 1571 the following occurs in the directions concerning the administration of baptism:

"The pastor shall stand by the head [of the child], and dip his head three times entirely under water, at first with the words, 'N., I baptize thee in the name of God the Father;' a second time, 'and of the Son;' the third time, 'and of the Holy Spirit.' And the sponsors shall stand on both sides and hold the child by the arms, and as oft as the priest immerses him draw him out again and raise him up."[165]

The Council of Besançon, in 1571, made this enactment:

"The custom of the church is to be observed in baptism as to immersion or aspersion, to wit: where it is the custom to immerse the child in water, he shall be immersed, unless there should be a reasonable apprehension concerning the life [of the child]; and where it is the custom to sprinkle or pour water upon the head, without immersion, that also shall be observed."[166]

The Austrian church *Agenda* of 1571 has the following direction:

"As then the nurse or another woman shall unloose the child, and the minister shall take the same in his hand, the sponsors holding the child's hands and head, the priest with the other hand shall sprinkle water copiously thrice on the child, disrobed, saying very slowly, clearly, and distinctly, with intelligible voice, the following words, with especial earnestness and seriousness: 'N., I baptize thee,'" etc.[167]

In the second series of the *Zurich Letters* (Parker

Society, 1845, p. 356) there is a paper, written about 1575 by Bishop Horn of England to Henry Bullinger, the successor of Zwingli as pastor in Zurich, which has the following reference to the act of baptism in the Church of England in the time of Edward VI.:

"If there are any infants to be baptized, they are brought on each Sunday, when the most people are come together to the morning or evening prayers. The minister reads an exhortation to the people, in which he teaches them what is the condition of those who are not born again in Christ, and what the sacrament of regeneration signifies. He adds with the church a prayer for the infant, rehearses the gospel from the tenth chapter of Mark, upon which he makes a brief exhortation, followed by a general giving of thanks. The godfathers and godmothers then approach, and demand the sacrament in the name of the infant. The minister examines them concerning their faith, and afterward dips the infant in the water, saying, 'I baptize thee,'" etc.

Carlo Borromeo, Archbishop of Milan, 1576, gave this direction concerning baptism:

"Let the rite of baptism be carefully observed, but let there be no confusion. Let baptism be so administered as the custom of the church, approved by the bishop, demands, whether it be by pouring or by immersion."[168]

For the Milan church, however, he insisted upon immersion. In Borromeo's ritual we find the following:

"Baptism is administered in three ways—by immersion, pouring, or sprinkling of water. But since it is claimed that the mode and rite of immersion is a most ancient institution in the holy church of God, and has always been retained in the church of God, and has always been retained in the Ambrosian Church, it is not permitted to depart from the custom of immersion unless there is imminent peril of death; and then it is to be administered either by the pouring or sprinkling of water, the established form of baptism being preserved."[169]

Concerning the administration of baptism by immersion, he says:

"The administrator, in immersing, will take care to stand at that part of the font where by direct vision he looks to the east. In the immersion he will see to it that, holding the sides of the infant firmly with both hands, he thrice immerses the back part of his head, face downward, first saying, 'In the name of the Father;' then, 'and of the Son;' and third, 'of the Holy Spirit.' In the immersion

THE ACT OF BAPTISM. 153

he will take care that he may not injure the child, but that the water really touches the back part of its head in the immersion." [170]

In the ritual the direction is as follows:

"The administrator receives the infant, face downward, from the sponsor, supported by both hands, so that the right may be nearer his head; then he thrice immerses the back part of his head in water, in the form of a cross, and in the immersion, if he certainly knows that he has not been baptized, he says plainly, 'N., I baptize thee in the name of the Father, and of the Son, and of the Holy Spirit. Amen.' These words are said while he thrice immerses: once when he says, 'N., I baptize thee in the name of the Father;' again while he says, 'and of the Son;' and thirdly, while he says, 'and of the Holy Spirit. Amen.'" [171]

That the font in the baptistery at Parma was used for immersion is proved by a report which was forwarded to the pope, Nov. 21, 1578:

"In the same church is a baptistery, and there are fonts separate from the baptistery.

"For the consecration of the sacred font the parish priests of the city do not convene.

"The office of baptizing belongs to two priests who are called *dogmani;* yet they do not baptize, but have a substitute, who supplies their places.

"They baptize by immersion."[172]

At Orleans there is a ritual of 1581, in which trine immersion is prescribed:

"The presbyter says to the child, 'And I baptize thee in the name of the Father' (immerses once), 'and of the Son' (immerses a second time), 'and of the Holy Spirit. Amen' (immerses a third time)."[173]

The Council of Bourges, in 1584, made this requirement:

"Those administering baptism shall observe either trine immersion or affusion."[174]

The Lower Saxon ritual of 1585 has the following direction:

"Then let him take the child and dip it in the font or . . . sprinkle it with water."[175]

The second Bamberg *Agenda*, 1587, made this declaration:

"It would be safer and more prudent to sprinkle the child thrice with a little water than to immerse him in water."[176]

The Saxon *Visitation Articles* of 1592, in Art. iii., "Of Holy Baptism," contain the following:

"1. That there is but one baptism and one ablution—not that which is used to take away the filth of the body, but that which washes us from our sins.

THE ACT OF BAPTISM. 155

"2. By baptism, as a bath of the regeneration and renovation of the Holy Ghost, God saves us and works in us such justice and purgation from our sins that he who perseveres to the end in that covenant and hope does not perish, but has eternal life.

"3. All who are baptized in Jesus Christ are baptized in his death, and by baptism are buried with him in his death and have put on Christ.

"4. Baptism is the bath of regeneration, because in it we are born again and sealed by the Spirit of adoption through grace (or gratuitously)." [177]

In the Strasburg ritual of 1598 occurs the following:

"Let the minister take the child and ask what it shall be named. Then let him sprinkle water thrice upon his head, and say, 'N., I baptize thee,'" etc. [178]

In the Prayer-book of James I. of England, 1604, called the *Hampton Court-book*, the directions for baptism are as follows:

"Then the priest shall take the child in his hands, and naming the child shall dip it in the water, so it be discreetly and warily done; . . . and if the child shall be weak, it shall suffice to pour water upon it."

In the *Anglican Catechism*, edition of 1604, occurred the following question and answer concerning baptism:

"*Ques.*—What is the outward visible sign or form of baptism?

"*Ans.*—Water. The person baptized is dipped or sprinkled with it in the name of the Father, and of the Son, and of the Holy Ghost."

In the English ritual prepared in 1604 for the use of the English seminary at Douay, in Flanders, the priest is directed to take the infant presented for baptism and administer the ordinance as follows:

"He shall dip him once, with his face toward the west, and say, 'I baptize thee in the name of the Father;' then he shall dip him again, with his face toward the south, and shall say, 'and of the Son;' and then he shall dip him a third time, with his face toward the water, and shall say, 'and of the Holy Ghost. Amen.'"

In the Venetian *Order of Baptism*, 1612, occurs the following:

"'I baptize thee in the name of the Father +, and of the Son +, and of the Holy Spirit +, Amen,' at each cross pouring the water of baptism over the head of the baptized."[179]

In the Roman ritual put forth by Pope Paul

THE ACT OF BAPTISM. 157

V. in 1614 for use in the Romish Church is this injunction concerning baptism:

"Either the godfather or godmother, or both (if both are admitted), holding the infant, the priest takes baptismal water in a small vessel or pitcher, and from it thrice pours over the head of the infant, in the form of a cross; and at the same time uttering the words once only, distinctly and carefully, he says, 'I baptize thee in the name of the Father +' (pours once), 'and of the Son +' (pours a second time), 'and of the Holy Spirit +' (pours a third time)."[180]

In the ritual, however, Pope Paul deems it necessary to mention immersion; and gives the following directions in reference to the baptism of infants by this mode:

"Where it is the custom to baptize by immersion, the priest takes the infant; and exercising care lest it be injured, he immerses its head and baptizes it with trine immersion, and says once only, 'N.,'" etc.[181]

The direction of the baptism for adults is as follows:

"But in those churches where baptism is by immersion either of the whole body or only of the head, the priest takes the elect by the arms, near the shoulders, . . . and by thrice immersing him, or his head, baptizes him, invoking the holy Trinity once only."[182]

Rev. Dr. Featley, in his *Clavis Mystica*, which was published in 1536, says:

"Our font is always open, or ready to be opened, and the minister attends to receive the children of the faithful, and to dip them in that sacred laver."

The Scotch liturgy of 1637, in its reference to baptism, is like the book of Edward VI. of England, 1552, which prescribed single immersion, except "the child be weak," in which case pouring was allowed.

The Magdeburg *Agenda* of 1632 contains the following direction:

"Then let him take the child and sprinkle water thrice on it, and say, 'And I baptize thee,'" etc.[183]

In the Nuremberg *Agenda* of 1639 occurs the following:

"Then let him take the child and baptize it with water, and say, 'And I baptize thee,'" etc.[184]

In 1641, Edward Barber, once a minister of the Established Church in England, but then a minister of a Baptist church in the Spittle, Bishopsgate Street, London, was sentenced to eleven months' imprisonment for the publication of a book with this title:

A Treatise on Baptism, or Dipping; wherein is already showed that our Lord Jesus Christ ordained dipping, and that sprinkling of children is not according to Christ's institution; and also the invalidity of those arguments which are commonly brought to justify that practice.

Luke Howard, who had joined the Baptists in England, and afterward, renouncing his Baptist sentiments, had become a Quaker, wrote a book entitled *Looking-glass for Baptists* (see Goadby's *Bye-Paths in Baptist History*, p. 36), in which he says:

"In the years 1643–1644 the people called Baptists began to have an entrance into Kent; and Ann Stevens, of Canterbury, who was afterward my wife, being the first that received them there, was dipped into the belief and church of William Kiffin, who then was of the opinion commonly called the particular election and reprobation of persons; and by him was also dipped Nicholas Woodman of Canterbury, myself, and Mark Elfrith of Dover, with many more, both men and women, who were all of the opinion on that particular point, and also reckoned themselves of the seven churches in that day who gave forth a book called *The Faith of the Seven Churches*, which was the opposite to the Baptists that held the general, as is still the same." He refers to the Particular and the General Baptists.

The Confession of Faith of Seven Congregations or Churches of Christ in London, which are commonly, but unjustly, called Anabaptists, adopted in 1643 and printed in London in 1646, has the following articles concerning baptism:

"39. Baptism is an ordinance of the New Testament, given by Christ, to be dispensed upon persons professing faith or that are made disciples, who, upon profession of faith, ought to be baptized, and after to partake of the Lord's Supper.

"40. That the way and manner of the dispensing this ordinance is dipping or plunging the body under water; it, being a sign, must answer to the thing signified, which is that interest the saints have in the death, burial, and resurrection of Christ; and that, as certainly as the body is buried under water and risen again, so certainly shall the bodies of the saints be raised by the power of Christ, in the day of the resurrection, to reign with Christ."

In 1644, Rev. Thomas Blake of Tamworth, in Staffordshire, England, in a work entitled *The Birth Privilege* (p. 33), says:

"I have been an eye-witness of many infants dipped, and I know it to have been the constant practice of many ministers in their places for many years together."

In another passage he says:

"Those that dip not infants do not yet use to sprinkle them: there is a middle way between these two. I have seen several dipped; I never saw nor heard of any sprinkled, or (as some of you use to speak) *rantized*. . . . Our way is not by *aspersion*, but perfusion; not sprinkling drop by drop, but pouring on, at once, all that the hand contains."

In the same year, the Presbyterians having gained the ascendency in England under the Protectorate of Oliver Cromwell, an assembly of divines, known as the Westminster Assembly, which met in London, prepared a *Directory*, in which was the following in reference to the administration of baptism:

"The minister shall take water and sprinkle or pour it with his hand upon the face or forehead of the child."

Some were not satisfied with this statement. Dr. Lightfoot, one of the most prominent in the discussion that followed, kept a journal of the proceedings of the assembly, and in his account of the discussion, August 7, 1644, he says (*Works*, Lond., 1824, vol. xiii., pp. 300, 301):

"Then fell we upon the work of the day, which was about baptizing of the child—whether to dip or sprinkle him. And this proposition, 'It is lawful and sufficient to besprinkle the child,' had been canvassed before our adjourning, and was ready now to vote. But I spoke against it as being very unfit to vote that it is lawful to sprinkle when every one grants it. Whereupon it was fallen upon, sprinkling being granted, whether dipping should be tolerated with it. And here fell we upon a large and long discourse whether dipping were essential or used in the first institution or in the Jews' custom. Mr. Coleman went about in a large discourse to prove *tauveleh* to be 'dipping over head,' which I answered at large. After a long dispute it was at last put to the question whether the *Directory* should run: 'The minister shall take water, and sprinkle or pour it with his hand upon the face or forehead of the child;' and it was voted so indifferently that we were glad to count names twice; for so many were unwilling to have dipping excluded that the vote came to an equality, within one, for the one side was twenty-four, the other twenty-five, the twenty-four for the reserving of dipping, and the twenty-five against it. And then grew a great heat upon it; and when we had done all, we concluded upon nothing in it, but the business was recommitted."

On the following day, after further discussion, it was decided that the *Directory* should read:

"He is to baptize the child with water, which, for the manner of so doing, is not only lawful, but also sufficient and most expedient, to be by pouring or sprinkling water on the face of the child, without any other ceremony."

In harmony with this action of the Westminster Assembly was the requirement forbidding the child to be carried to the font:

"Baptism is to be administered, not in private places or privately, but in the place of public worship and in the face of the congregation, and not in the places where fonts, in the time of popery, were unfitly or superstitiously placed."

Wall (*History of Infant Baptism*, vol. ii., p. 312) says:

"The use was: The minister continuing in his reading-desk, the child was brought and held below him, and there was placed for that use a little basin of water about the size of a syllabub-pot; into which the minister dipping his fingers, and then holding his hand over the face of the child, some drops would fall from his fingers on the child's face."

REMARKS.

During the fourteenth century immersion was still the rule in the administration of baptism. Concerning the practice in England, we have a glimpse in a manuscript life of Richard, Earl of Warwick, which was illustrated by John Rouse, who died January 14, 1491. One of these illustrations represents the baptism of Richard in 1381, and a copy of the illustration will be found in Robinson's *History of Baptism* (1st London ed., p. 127) and in Cote's *Archæology of Baptism* (p. 237). The description, as given by Robinson, is as follows:

"Round a neat Saxon font the company stood. A bishop is holding the child, stark naked and just going to be dipped, over the font. The hand of the royal godfather is on his head. The archdeacon, according to custom, stands by the bishop, holding up the service-book, open, which implies that the baptism is being performed according to the ritual. As the child's face is toward the water, this is the last of the three immersions, and the bishop may be supposed now uttering the last clause of the baptismal words, 'And of the Holy Ghost. Amen.'"

This is also a good illustration of baptism as administered on the Continent in the fourteenth century, though the new practice was gradually winning favor in the Latin Church. But by the middle of the fifteenth century sprinkling and pouring had become common, except in the Greek Church, which continued the ancient practice.

In England, at the opening of the sixteenth century, immersion was still the rule. The rituals in use previous to the middle of this century give no sanction to sprinkling or pouring in public baptism. The first instance of such a sanction is found in the Prayer-book of Edward VI., in which three dippings are commanded, with this exception, that "if the child be weak, it shall suffice to pour water upon it."

In Germany, at the opening of the Reformation, sprinkling or pouring had obtained very general recognition, though in the northern part immersion was still the prevailing practice.[185] The older Protestant liturgies give the preference to immersion, as did Luther and other of the Reformers. The Anabaptists gave their attention at first wholly to the subjects of baptism. Not until 1525 do we find any protest on their part against pouring or sprinkling as practised in the Romish or Reformed churches. And this protest was confined to a limited number. In all the discussion which occurred between the Anabaptists and the Reformers, we find no dispute in reference to the act of baptism. Indeed, Luther could say, "Our Anabaptists acknowledge that the baptism practised by us and the Papists is undoubtedly right; but because it is given by unworthy persons, and received by unworthy persons, it is no baptism." Accordingly we find that the Anabaptists of the Reformation period and related bodies, like the Mennonites, acquiesced, for the most part, in the practice of the Romish and Reformed churches.

Calvin recognized only pouring in his *Form of Administering the Sacraments*. The English exiles on the Continent, through his influence, adopted the doctrine and practice of the Genevan Church, and on their return to England introduced the new form of baptism. Wall, in his *History of Infant Baptism* (vol. ii., pp. 308–310), says: "Pouring was not in Queen Mary's time used but in case of necessity. But there are apparent reasons why that custom should alter during Queen Elizabeth's reign." The first refers to the latitude allowed in the liturgy of Edward VI., and adds: "Another thing that had a greater influence than this was that many of our English divines and other people had, during Queen Mary's bloody reign, fled into Germany, Switzerland, etc.; and coming back in Queen Elizabeth's time, they brought with them a great love to the customs of those Protestant churches wherein they had sojourned; and especially the authority of Calvin, and the rules which he had established at Geneva, had a mighty influence on a great number of our people about that time. . . . And when there was added to all this the resolution of such a man as Dr. Whitaker, Regius Professor at Cambridge —'Though in case of grown persons that are in health I think dipping to be better, yet in the case of infants and of sickly people I think sprinkling sufficient'— the inclination of the people, backed with these authorities, carried the practice against the Rubric, which still required dipping, except in case of weakness, so that in the later times of Queen Elizabeth and during the reigns of King James and of King Charles I. very few children were dipped in the font."

This change was not brought about without a struggle on the part of some who resisted the change from the font to the basin. In the preface to his valuable work On *Baptismal Fonts,* Simpson says: "From the time of the Reformation to the days of Puritanic fury in the reign of Charles I., there was a strong propensity to remove or neglect the font and use a basin instead. This was checked so long as it was possible. Thus in 1565 it was directed 'that the fonte be not removed, nor the curate do baptize in the parishe churches in any basins, nor in any other forme than is alreadie prescribed.' In 1570, it was directed: '*Curabunt (Æditui) ut in singulis ecclesiis sit sacer fons, non pelvis, in quo baptismus ministretur, isque ut decenter et munde conservetur.*' [They will take care (the Æditui) that in each church there may be a sacred font—not a basin—in which baptism may be administered, etc.] Again, the eighty-first canon of 1603 says: 'According to a former constitution, too much neglected in many places, we appoint that there shall be a font of stone in every church and chapel where baptism is to be ministered, the same to be set in the ancient usual places. In which only font the minister shall baptize publicly.' Among the inquiries directed to be made by the churchwardens, one is whether the font has been removed from its accustomed place, and whether they use a basin or other vessel."

This resistance was of little avail. Immersion gradually disappeared, largely through the influence of the returned exiles, especially in Scotland. Thus it was that James I., the successor of Elizabeth, favored the substitution of sprinkling for immersion in England. Later, during the Protectorate, when, in the Westminster Assembly, the question was before that body of divines whether in the *Directory*, in the article relating to baptism, there should be any reference to immersion, the vote on the first division stood twenty-four to twenty-five. The subject was then recommitted, and on the following day—but by what vote we are not told—an article was adopted omitting any reference to immersion. This was in the Presbyterian Church. In the Church of England the ritual remained unchanged, retaining the direction for dipping, which year by year, however, was less and less observed.

But already in England there were bodies of Christians in which the observance of apostolic baptism—the immersion of a believer in water—was insisted upon. Their Confession of Faith, adopted in 1643, restored the ancient practice, when from other Confessions it was rapidly disappearing.

In the Romish Church, at the close of this period, immersion was practised in some places; but such practice was the exception, not the rule.

CHAPTER VI.

FROM THE WESTMINSTER ASSEMBLY TO THE PRESENT TIME.

A. D. 1644–1879.

OF the practice of the Baptists in England, Dr. Featley, who wrote in 1645, says, in the preface to his *Dippers Dipped:*

"This fire, which in the reigns of Queen Elizabeth and King James, and our gracious sovereign [Charles I.] till now, was covered in England under the ashes; or if it brake out at any time, by the care of the ecclesiastical and civil magistrates it was soon put out. But of late, since the unhappy distractions which our sins have brought upon us, the temporal sword being otherways employed, and the spiritual locked up fast in the scabbard, this sect, among others, has so far presumed upon the patience of the state that it hath held weekly conventicles, rebaptized hundreds of men and women together in the twilight in rivulets and some arms of the Thames, and elsewhere, dipping them over head and ears."

The *Westminster Confession of Faith*, 1647, in chapter xxviii., 3, made this declaration:

"Dipping of the person into water is not necessary; but baptism is rightly administered by pouring or sprinkling water upon the person."

In his *Sum and Substance of the Christian Religion* (6th ed., p. 413), Archbishop Usher, who died in 1656, says:

"Some there are that stand strictly for the particular action of diving or dipping the baptized under the water as the only action which the institution of the sacrament will bear; and our church allows no other, except in case of the child's weakness; and there is expressed in our Saviour's baptism both the descending into the water and the rising up."

In a *Confession* adopted by some Baptist churches in Somerset, England, and some churches in adjacent counties, which was published in London in 1656, we read in Article xxiv. as follows:

"That it is the duty of every man and woman that have repented from dead works, and have faith toward God, to be baptized—that is, dipped or buried under the water—in the name of our Lord Jesus, or in the name of the Father, Son, and Holy Spirit, therein to signify and represent a washing away of sin, and their death, burial, and resurrection with Christ."

In Book iii. (chap. iv., rule 15) of his *Doctor Dubitantium*, or *Rule of Conscience*, published in 1660, Jeremy Taylor says:

"This is the sense and law of the Church of England—not that it be indifferent, but that all infants be dipped, except in the case of sickness, and then sprinkling is permitted."

In 1660, *A Brief Confession or Declaration of Faith, lately presented to King Charles the Second, Set Forth by many of us who are Falsely called Anabaptists*, was published in London. In Article xi. we read:

"That the right and only way of gathering churches (according to Christ's appointment, Matt. xxviii. 19, 20) is first to teach or preach the gospel (Mark xvi. 16) to the sons and daughters of men, and then to *baptize*—that is, in *English, to dip*—in the name of the Father, Son, and Holy Spirit, or in the name of the Lord Jesus Christ, such only of them as profess repentance toward God and faith toward our Lord Jesus Christ."

In the *Anglican Catechism*, edition of 1604, the question, "What is the outward visible sign or form in baptism?" was answered, "Water, wherein the person baptized is dipped, or sprinkled with it, in the name of the Father, and of the Son, and of the Holy Ghost." In the edition of 1661, however, instead of the words, "the person baptized is dipped or sprinkled with it," occur the words, "the person is baptized."

In the Prayer-book, as revised and settled at the Savoy Conference, under Charles II., in 1662, we find the following:

"Then the priest shall take the child into his hands, and shall say to the godfathers and godmothers, 'Name this child.' And then, naming it after them (if they shall certify him that the child may well endure it), he shall dip it in the water discreetly and warily, saying, 'N., I baptize thee in the name of the Father, and of the Son, and of the Holy Ghost. Amen.' But if they certify that the child is weak, it shall suffice to pour water upon it, saying the foresaid words."

The Weimar ritual of 1664 has the following direction:

"Then let him take the infant in the left hand and sprinkle it upon the back or head thrice."[186]

In 1678, a Confession of Faith containing fifty articles was adopted by fifty-four ministers and messengers of Baptist churches in Bucks, Hertford, Bedford, and Oxford Counties, England.

THE ACT OF BAPTISM. 173

Concerning the act of baptism, this Confession, Article xxviii., says:

"And orderly ought none to be admitted into the visible church of Christ without being first baptized; and those which do really profess repentance toward God, and faith in and obedience to our Lord Jesus Christ, are the only proper subjects of this ordinance, according to our Lord's holy institution and primitive practice; and ought by the minister or administrator to be done in a solemn manner, in the name of the Father, Son, and Holy Ghost, by immersion, or dipping of the person in the element of water, this being necessary to the due administration of this holy sacrament, as holy Scripture sheweth, and the first and best antiquity witnesseth for some centuries of years."

Dr. Towerson, in his work *On the Sacraments*, published in London, in 1686 (p. 24), considers immersion the only legitimate rite of baptism, and adds:

"Our church hath acquitted itself from all blame, because manifestly licensing the sprinkling of infants with respect to the weakness of their state; and I have the more carefully noted both that and the ground of our practice, the better to defend ourselves from a retort of the

Romanists when we charge them with sacrilege in the matter of the Eucharist for taking away the cup from the laity. For why not (as they sometimes answer), as well as change the rite of immersion in baptism into that of sprinkling, especially when a great part of the symbolicalness of that sacrament lies in the manner of the application of its sign? Which answer of theirs were not, in my opinion, easy to be repelled, were it not that we have that necessity to justify our practice, which they cannot pretend for their own."

Dean Comber, in his work *On the Common Prayer*, published in London, in 1688 (p. 197), says:

"Because the way of immersion was the most ancient, our church doth first prescribe that, and only permits the other where it is certified the child is weak, although custom has now prevailed to the laying the first wholly aside."

Selden, in his *Table-Talk*, published in 1689, says (vol. iii., p. 2008):

"In England, of late years, I ever thought the parson baptized his own fingers rather than the child."

The London *Confession* of 1689, put forth by the ministers and messengers of more than one hun-

THE ACT OF BAPTISM. 175

dred Baptist churches in England and Wales, has this direction in chapter xxix., "On Baptism:"

"The outward element to be used in this ordinance is water, wherein the party is to be baptized in the name of the Father, and of the Son, and of the Holy Spirit. Immersion, or dipping of the person in water, is necessary to the due administration of the ordinance."

Baxter, who died in 1691, in his *Dispu. of Right to Sac.* (2d London ed., p. 70), says:

"It is commonly confessed by us to the Anabaptists, as our commentators declare, that in the apostles' time the baptized were dipped over head in the water, and that this signified their profession, both of believing the burial and resurrection of Christ and of their own present renouncing the world and flesh, or dying to sin and living to Christ, or rising again to newness of life, or being buried and risen again with Christ, as the apostle expoundeth in the forecited texts of Col. and Rom. And though (as before said) we have thought it lawful to disuse the manner of dipping, and to use less water, yet we presume not to change the use and signification of it."

Also, in his *Plain Scripture Proof* (part ii., chap. xii., p. 134, 3d London ed.), Baxter says:

"For my own part, I may say, as Mr. Blake,

that I never saw a child sprinkled, but all that I have seen baptized had water poured on them, and so were washed."

Dr. Sharp, Archbishop of York, in his sermon before Queen Mary, March 27, 1692, said:

"Whenever a person in ancient times was baptized, he was not only to profess his faith in Christ's death and resurrection, but he was also to look upon himself as obliged, in correspondence therewith, to mortify his former carnal affections, and so enter upon a new state of life; and the very form of baptism did lively represent this obligation to them. For what did their being plunged under water signify but their undertaking, in imitation of Christ's death and burial, to forsake all their former evil courses, as their ascending out of the water did their engagement to lead a holy spiritual life?"

John de Saint Valier, Bishop of Quebec, published in 1703 a ritual for the use of his diocese. It recognizes two kinds of baptism—by immersion, in which case the whole body of the infant is plunged into the water, and by affusion, in which case a small quantity of water is poured upon the infant's head. In the latter case the water is poured three times, in the form of a cross, from a small vessel.[187]

Wall, in his *History of Infant Baptism*, published in 1707, gives this testimony (vol. ii., chap. ix., p. 310):

"I have heard of one or two persons now living, who must have been born in those reigns [King James and Charles I.], that they were baptized by dipping in the font, and of one clergyman now living that has baptized some infants so, but am not certain.—P. S. I have since heard of several. And I myself have had an opportunity of administering baptism so by the parents' request. But the children were, however, all that time carried to the font; as much as to say, 'The minister is ready to dip the child if the parents will venture the health of it.'"

Benedictus XIII., who was elected pope in 1724, desirous, among other reforms in ecclesiastical matters, of returning to the ancient rite of immersion, caused a baptistery to be constructed in the chapel of John the Baptist, in Rome. A marble slab in the rear of the font reads as follows:

"Benedict XIII., supreme pontiff of the Order of Preachers, constructed this font of human regeneration for the ancient rite in the year of salvation 1725, the second year of his pontificate."[188]

In 1736, a Maronite synod, held in Mount Lebanon, decreed as follows:

"The Holy Synod strictly enjoins that hereafter no one shall use any other form than that which is prescribed in the approved ritual, nor shall any other ceremonies be used in the administration of this sacrament, except those which, established by our ancestors and handed down to us, are preserved in the Oriental Church; so that most surely, when the child has been stripped of all his clothing, the priest shall receive it carefully and baptize it by trine immersion by burying the whole of its body, at the same time invoking the most holy Trinity and saying, 'I baptize thee in the name of the Father' (and let him immerse it once and lift it up out of the water), 'and of the Son' (and let him immerse it a second time and lift it out), 'and of the Holy Ghost' (and let him immerse it a third time and lift it out); and let the deacon at every immersion respond, 'Amen.' But where adults are to be baptized, and especially women who cherish modesty and honor, we do not permit that they, according to ancient custom, shall be stripped of their garments and immersed in a baptistery, as we have above decreed concerning children; but we determine they shall lay bare

THE ACT OF BAPTISM. 179

the head alone, and that the priest shall pour water upon their heads once, saying, 'I baptize thee in the name of the Father;' and again, saying, 'and of the Son;' and a third time, saying, 'and of the Holy Ghost.' This rite of pouring water upon the head, or even of immersing the head alone in water, the priest may use according to the custom of the place. But he shall use it especially when, were the candidate wholly immersed in the water, his life would be endangered." [189]

In John Wesley's *Journal*, which covers the period from his embarkation for Georgia until his return to London, there is the following record (*Works*, vol. i., p. 130) of a baptism at Savannah in 1736:

"*Saturday, 21st February.*—Mary Welch, aged eleven days, was baptized, according to the custom of the first church and the rule of the Church of England, by immersion."

Another record (*Works*, vol. i., p. 134) is as follows:

"*Wednesday, May 5th.*—I was asked to baptize a child of Mr. Parker, second bailiff of Savannah. But Mrs. Parker told me, 'Neither Mr. Parker nor I will consent to its being dipped.' I answered, 'If you certify that your child is weak, it will suffice, the Rubric says, to pour water upon it.' She replied: 'Nay, the child is not weak; but I am resolved it shall not be dipped.' This argument I could not confute. So I went home, and the child was baptized by another person."

Bernard Picart, in his *Les Cérémonies et Coutumes Réligieuses*, published at Amsterdam in 1736 (vol. vi., pp. 222, 223, English ed.), thus describes the rite of baptism as administered by the Rhynsburgers, or Collegiants, a branch of the Mennonites originating in Holland:

"The candidate for baptism makes publicly his profession of faith on a Saturday, in the morning, before an assembly of Rhynsburgers held for that purpose. A discourse is pronounced on the excellency and nature of baptism. The minister and candidate go together to a pond behind a house belonging to his sect (we might call it a hospital, since they received for nothing those who had not wherewithal to pay their hotel-bills). In that pond the neophyte, catechumen, or candidate is baptized by immersion. If a man, he has a waistcoat and drawers; if a woman, a bodice and petticoat, with leads in the hem, for the sake of decency. The minister, in the same dress as the men wear, is also in the water, and plunges them in it, pronouncing at the same time the form used by most Christian communities. This being over, they put on their clothes, go back to the meeting, hear an exhortation to perseverance in complying with the precepts of Christ; a public prayer is said and some hymns or psalms sung."

In his *Account of Baptism in the Russo-Greek Church* (vol. v., pp. 307, 308) Picart says:

"As soon as an infant comes into the world the parents send for a priest to purify it. This purification extends to all those who are present at the ceremony. They baptize their infants, according to Olearius, as soon as they are born; but according to other historians, those who are in good circumstances are not so strict, and defer the ceremony for some time. The godfathers and godmothers of the first child must stand sureties for all the other children in that family, however numerous they may be. After their entrance into the church the godfathers deliver nine wax tapers into the hands of the priest, who lights them all and sticks them, in the form of a cross, about the font or vessel in which the infant is to be baptized. The priest purifies the godfathers and consecrates the water; after that he and the godfathers go thrice in procession round it. The clerk, who marches in the front, carries the image of John the Baptist. They then all range themselves in such a manner that their backs are turned toward the font, as a testimony, says Olearius, of their aversion to the three questions which the priest proposes to the godfathers—that is to say, (1) whether the child renounces the devil, (2) whether he abjures his angels, and (3) whether he abhors and detests their impious works. At each question the godfathers answer 'Yes,' and spit upon the ground. The exorcism follows, which is performed out of the church, lest the devil, as he comes out of the infant, should pollute or profane it. The baptism which ensues is performed by triple immersion. . . . Proselytes to the Russian religion are baptized in some rapid stream or adjacent river. They are plunged therein three times successively; and if it happens in the winter season, a hole is made in the ice for the performance of the ordinance. If, however, a person is of too weak a constitution to undergo immersion, a barrelful of water is poured over his head three times, one after another."

Concerning baptism in the Abyssinian Church (vol. v., p. 236), Picart says:

"The mother, dressed in her best clothes, attends at the church door with her infant in her arms. Then the priest who officiates pronounces several long prayers for a blessing on them both, beginning with those peculiarly appropriate to the mother. Afterward he conducts them into the church, and anoints the infant six times with the oil consecrated for exorcisms. . . . As soon as the benediction of the font is over he plunges the infant into it three times successively. At the first he dips one-third part of the infant's body into the water, saying, 'I baptize thee in the name of the Father;' he then dips him lower, about two-thirds, adding, 'I baptize thee in the name of the Son;' the third time he plunges him all over, saying, 'I baptize thee in the name of the Holy Ghost.' . . . In case the infant should be sick, they bring it to the church and lay it on a cloth spread before the font, into which the priest dips his hands three times and rubs the infant all over with them, wet as they are, from head to foot."

The Strasburg ritual of 1742, under Cardinal Armandus Gasto von Rohan, recognized pouring only:

"No one baptizes in any other way than by trine affusion." [190]

Richard Pococke, in his *Compendium of Modern Travel* (vol. ii., p. 30), which was published in

London in 1743, has the following reference to baptism in the Coptic Church:

"The Coptic Church is something like the Greek Church in its ceremonies. At baptism they plunge the child three times into the water, and then confirm it and give it the sacrament—that is, the wine. . . . If the child happens to be sick before it is baptized, it is brought to church, for they cannot baptize out of the church; they lay the child on a cloth near the font, and the priest dips his hands in the water and rubs it all over. If the child is so ill that it cannot be brought to church, they then only anoint, according to the form they have for this purpose, which they say is good baptism."

The Ulm ritual of 1747 has the following direction:

"Then let the minister pour water thrice on the child, and say with clear, loud, distinct voice, 'N., I baptize thee,'" etc.[191]

The ritual of the Armenians unites affusion and immersion. The following was translated from the original into Latin by Assemani, and is found in his *Codex Liturgicus Ecclesiæ Universæ*, which was published 1749–1763:

"He [the priest] then places the infant in the font and pours with his hand some water upon his head, saying, 'N. is baptized in the name of the Father, and of the Son, and of the Holy Ghost; redeemed by the blood of Christ from the slavery of sin, he obtains the liberty of the adoption of the children of our heavenly Father, that he may become joint-heir with Christ and a temple of the Holy Ghost, now and for ever, and to ages of ages.' This he says thrice, and immerses him three times, burying in the water the sins of the old man, and in order to represent the three days' burial of Christ and his resurrection. He then washes the whole body, and says, 'As many of you as have been baptized into Christ have put on Christ. Hallelujah. As many of you as have been illuminated in the Father, the Holy Ghost shall rejoice in you.'"

In June, 1770, the first Assembly of Free-grace General Baptists in England adopted articles of faith, of which the sixth, "On Baptism," was as follows:

"We believe that it is the indispensable duty of all who repent and believe the gospel to be baptized by immersion in water, in order to be initiated into a church-state, and that no person ought to be received into the church without submission to this ordinance."

The Bamberg *Instructional* of 1773 says:

"Baptism may be administered either by affusion, or immersion, or sprinkling; nevertheless, the prevailing mode—namely, affusion—should be retained, according to the custom of the church of the present time, so that with trine and not single ablution the head and not the breast of the baptized should be poured over."[192]

The Protestant Episcopal Church in the American colonies, so long as they were under the government of the mother-country, formed a part of the English Church and used the English Prayer-book. But in 1789, after the recognition of the independence of the colonies, the Episcopal Church in the United States made certain alterations in the Rubric, one of which was in the office for the public baptism of infants. The amended Rubric read as follows:

"And then, naming it after them, he shall dip it in the water discreetly, and shall pour water upon it, saying, 'N., I baptize thee,'" etc.

Robinson, in his *History of Baptism*, published in London, in 1790 (Boston, 1817, pp. 487, 488), describes a baptism in one of the Calvinist Congregational churches in England. In the address before the baptism the minister remarked:

"Dipping was not necessary, but baptism was rightly administered by pouring or sprinkling.

THE ACT OF BAPTISM. 187

". . . After prayer, the fathers presented the children one by one, and the minister, taking the child into his arms, dipped his fingers' ends in the water, sprinkled it on the face of the babe, said in the mean time, 'I baptize thee,'" etc.

Bishop William White, of the Protestant Episcopal Church in the United States, who was consecrated in 1789, when the alterations of the Rubric, noticed above, were made, in his *Lectures on the Catechism*, published in Philadelphia, in 1813, says (p. 363), in a reference to the question as to immersion or affusion:

"The result, in the estimation of him who now writes, is that the present general practice is a deviation from what it was originally, which it is desirable to restore to the standard of the Rubrics as they were framed in the Church of England, and as they continue to this day in the liturgy of that and of the American Church, although fallen by universal custom into neglect."

Alexander de Stourdza, a Greek of Odessa, published, in 1816, a work entitled *Considerations on the Doctrine and Spirit of the Orthodox Church*. In reference to the doctrinal teachings of the Greek Church, it is recognized by scholars as a standard work. Concerning baptism (p. 85), he says:

"The distinctive character of the rite of baptism is, then, immersion, *baptisma*, which cannot be omitted without destroying the mysterious meaning of the sacrament and contradicting, at the same time, the etymological signification of the word which seems to designate it.

"The church of the West has, therefore, turned aside from following Jesus Christ, she has put out of sight all the sublimity of the external sign—in fine, she has done violence both to the word and to the idea—in practising baptism by sprinkling, the bare mention of which is nothing less than a ludicrous contradiction. In fact, the verb $\beta\alpha\pi\tau\acute{\iota}\zeta\omega$, *immergo*, has only one meaning. It signifies literally and perpetually to plunge. Baptism and immersion are, therefore, identical, and to say 'baptism by sprinkling' is as if one should say 'immersion by sprinkling' or any other like self-contradictory expression."[193] Who would, after this statement, refuse his assent or hesitate to pay homage to the wise fidelity of our church, always immovably attached to the dogmatic tradition and ritual of primitive Christianity? She also has preserved the profound sense as well as the imposing forms of the initiatory sacrament, and we have only to read in the annals of the first centuries the description of baptismal ceremonies through which the catechumens passed, in order to be struck with their perfect identity with our present rites.

"So simple and clear an agreement has surely not escaped the doctors and writers of the Roman Church. But they perhaps believe that it suffices to turn away the eyes from evidence, in order to destroy its effect. We will only quote here, in passing, the celebrated author of the *Génie du Christianisme*, who, in speaking of baptism, enlarges greatly on the practices of the primitive church in the administration of this sacrament. Now, these practices are exactly the same as those which are now observed by the orthodox church. Nevertheless, the apologist for the beauties of religion takes care to make no remark on this for the instruction of his readers. He even pushes his ill-faith (for we cannot suppose it ignorance) so far as to appear to admire at a distance these beautiful and ancient forms of baptism as having fallen into disuse. He speaks of them only as if they were obsolete practices, and he affects to doubt whether they are still in force. Can we suppose with any probability that M. de Chateaubriand could be ignorant of the truth? And if he were informed of it, is his reserve pardonable? Was he right in concealing from his readers that at the present hour nearly sixty millions of Christians yet adminster baptism in imitation of that of Jesus Christ, of the apostles, and according to the institutions of the primitive church?"

The *Declaration of the Congregational Union of England and Wales*, adopted at the annual meeting in 1833, has the following statement:

"They believe in the perpetual obligation of baptism, . . . to be administered to all converts to Christianity and all their children, by the application of water to the subject in the name of the Father, and of the Son, and of the Holy Ghost."

In order to meet a very general desire for a more exact statement of doctrines accepted by Baptists in the United States, especially in the Northern States, what is known as the *New Hampshire Baptist Confession* was drawn up by Rev. John Newton Brown and others, and adopted by the New Hampshire Baptist Convention in 1833. It received very general recognition as a clear and concise statement of doctrine and practice as maintained by Baptists. Article xiv. says:

"We believe that Christian baptism is the immersion in water of a believer into the name of the Father, and Son, and Holy Ghost, to show forth, in a solemn and beautiful emblem, our faith in the crucified, buried, and risen Saviour, with its effect in our death to sin and resurrection to a new life."

The *Confession of the Freewill Baptists* was adopted and issued by the general conference of the Freewill Baptists in 1834. In chap. xvii., which treats of the "Ordinances of the Gospel," Christian baptism is thus defined:

"This is the immersion of believers in water in the name of the Father, the Son, and the Holy Spirit, in which are represented the burial and resurrection of Christ, the death of Christians to the world, the washing of their souls from the pollution of sin, their rising to newness of life, their engagement to serve God, and their resurrection at the last day."

The Larger Catechism of the Græco-Russian Church, which is now the authoritative doctrinal standard of that church, was approved in 1839. Concerning baptism, it says:

"Baptism is a sacrament, in which a man who believes, having the body thrice plunged in water in the name of God the Father, the Son, and the Holy Ghost, dies to the carnal life of sin, and is born again of the Holy Ghost to a life spiritual and holy."

The question, "What is most essential in the

administration of baptism?" is answered as follows: "Trine immersion in water, in the name of the Father, and of the Son, and of the Holy Ghost."

In 1851, Rev. Isaac Williams, late a Fellow of Trinity College, Oxford, England, published a volume entitled *Plain Sermons on the Catechism*, in which (p. 194) he says:

"But in speaking of this, the outward element of 'water wherein the person is baptized,' as of so much importance, it is necessary to speak of a custom which now prevails—of sprinkling with water rather than immersion. For *baptism* more properly signifies *washing* or *dipping*—i. e., immersion in water. The reasons given for this change are that in the countries we read of in Scripture, from the warmth of the climate, bathing in water is commonly practised, and there is not the slightest danger or risk; but in our colder countries all that is intended by this outward sign is equally shown by the pouring of water. . . . Now, this and more to the same effect may be said for the 'pouring of water,' rather than 'dipping in water,' sufficient to satisfy any scrupulous mind, where mercy or charity requires it; but where they do not, it is better to adhere to the primitive custom, both because it was the ancient and general practice, and because it more fully bears out the fulness of the sign of washing. Moreover, immersion in water has always been considered to imply the death unto sin, the being buried with Christ, as the apostle says, in baptism (Rom. vi. 4; Col. ii. 1,2), as set forth also in those figures of old, when they seemed, as it were, overwhelmed and buried in the midst of the waves of the Red Sea; or when the ark of Noah was in the midst of waters above, below, and on every side, the windows of heaven pouring down the flood, and the fountains of the great deep opened below. In Naaman, also, there was immersion, even sevenfold, in the sacred stream. For these reasons this ought to be the rule in baptizing, and the sprinkling or pouring of water ought to be the exception to the rule. So you will find it in the Prayer-book, in the rules given for baptism. And every clergyman, it is to be hoped, will be glad to abide by these rules, whenever he has an opportunity of doing so."

In the same year, Rev. William Palmer, a brother of Sir Roundell Palmer, formerly Attorney-General of England, presented a memorial to the Patriarch of Constantinople in reference to the requirements of the Greek Church concerning baptism. He desired to unite with the Greek

Church, but he felt that he was excluded from its communion by the contradiction which it presented, the Russians, on the one hand, recognized his baptism in the Church of England and forbidding rebaptism, the Greeks, on the other hand, affirming that he was unbaptized and enjoining him to receive baptism. October 8, 1851, he was admitted to an audience with the Patriarch and certain bishops. The Patriarch, in his answer to the memorial, said: "There is only one baptism; if some others allow a different one, we know nothing of it; we do not accept it. Our church knows only one baptism, and this without any subtraction or addition or alteration whatever."

In Badger's *The Nestorians and their Rituals* (vol. ii., pp. 207, 208), published in London, in 1852, the baptismal service in use among the Nestorians is given, from which the following is an extract:

"Then they shall take him [the child] to the priest standing by the font, who shall place him therein, with his face to the east; and he shall dip him therein three times, saying at the first time, 'A. B., be thou baptized in the name of the Father.' R., 'Amen.' The second time: 'In the name of the Son.' R., 'Amen.' And at the third time: 'In the name of the Holy Ghost.' R., 'Amen.' In dipping him he shall dip him up to the neck, and then put his hand upon him, so that his head may be submerged. Then the priest shall take him out of the font and give him to the deacon."

In a volume, published in London, in 1853, containing essays on the *Orthodox Communion*, Rev. William Palmer says (p. 179.):

"The rule of the Anglican Church is to baptize children by immersion, unless it be certified that the child is too weak to bear it, in which case affusion is allowed. But the common practice is not even to ask for any such certificate, but to baptize by affusion, or rather by sprinkling. . . . Now, to say nothing of the omission of other important ceremonies, adjuncts of baptism, from the Anglican ritual, the writer is aware that there is a deep sense both in the immersion (signified by the very word baptism) and in the threefold repetition of that immersion, once at the name of each Person of the blessed Trinity. He is aware that to dispense with either the one or the other of these things without any real necessity is contrary to the custom of the whole Catholic Church for many ages; so that baptism so administered must be irregular and uncanonical, and any individual so administering it worthy of canonical punishments. And although St. Gregory the Great, also called 'Dialogus,' may have thought the Spaniards justifiable in using baptism with one immersion only (they using it in an orthodox sense, not to symbolize any heresy, but to oppose the heresy of some who drew a perverse argument for their separate substances in the three Persons of the Trinity from the three immersions in baptism), still he cannot see that either the Spaniards or Pope Gregory could rightly, without a council, authorize any departure from the universal custom and tradition of the church in such a matter."

In his *Christianity in Turkey*, published in 1854, Rev. H. G. O. Dwight, a Congregational missionary, referring to baptism among the Armenians (p. 11), says:

"Baptism is performed by triple immersion, also by pouring water afterward three times upon the head."

Bayard Taylor, in his *Travels in Greece and Russia*, published in 1859, describing a baptism according to the rite of the Greek Church which he witnessed in Athens, says (p. 59):

"With one hand the priest poured water plentifully on his head, then lifted him out and dipped him a second time; but instead of affusion, it was this time complete immersion. Placing his hand over the child's mouth and nose, he plunged it completely under three times in succession."

Macarius, Rector of the Ecclesiastical Academy of St. Petersburg, published in Paris, in 1860, a work entitled *Theologie Dogmatique Orthodoxe*, in which (vol. ii., p. 376) he says:

"By the word *baptism* is understood the sacrament by which sinful man, born with the taint of hereditary corruption from his first parents, is born again of water and the Holy Ghost (John iii. 5), or, to speak more particularly, in which the sinner, instructed in the Christian faith, immersed thrice in the water in the name of the Father, and of the Son, and of the Holy Ghost, is purified by divine grace from all sin, and becomes a new man, justified and sanctified."

On page 385 he adds:

"As to aspersion, the form in which the church of the West at this day ordinarily administers baptism, it should be observed that it was admitted anciently only as an exception to the rule, in cases of absolute necessity, and most of all for bedridden invalids (called *clinics*, from κλίνη, "a bed"), who were unable to be baptized by immersion; and it is to be noted that even in the third century this form of baptism was, among some, still a subject for dispute, to a certain class of whom St. Cyprian deemed it his duty to write, in order to remove their uneasiness, that the sacrament of baptism lost nothing of its force from being thus administered. So the orthodox church to this day, in acknowledging that aspersion in the administration of baptism diminishes nothing of the force or virtue of the sacrament, nevertheless admits this form only in cases of urgent need, and solely as an exception to the general rule."

In 1861, Rev. James Chrystal, a presbyter of the Protestant Episcopal Church in the United States, published *A History of the Modes of Christian Baptism*, in which he urged a return to the practice of immersion. On page 213 he says:

"It is evident—1. That if we restore immersion, we only restore what has ever been our theory so far back as the history of the Anglican Church extends. We correct only a late, and not primitive, practice. 2. Should we restore the trine immersion as the general practice, we shall have good reason to lay claim to the only mode which, so far as we can judge from all the testimony which the early church affords, can lay historically-at-

THE ACT OF BAPTISM. 199

tested claim to being the normal mode of the apostles."

Dr. Döllinger, of Munich, in his celebrated work, published in 1861, *Kirche und Kirchen* (s. 337), says:

"The fact that the Baptists are so numerous, or even the most numerous of all religious parties, in North America deserves all attention. They would, indeed, be yet more numerous, were not baptism, as well as the Lord's Supper, as to their sacramental significance, regarded in the Calvinistic world as something so subordinate that the inquiry after the original form appears to many as something indifferent, about which one need not much trouble himself. The Baptists are, however, in fact, from the Protestant standpoint, unassailable; since for their demand of baptism by submersion they have the clear Bible text, and the authority of the church and of her testimony is regarded by neither party."

The ritual now in use in the Greek Church is as follows:

"Let the priest baptize him, holding him erect; and looking toward the east, let the priest say: 'The servant of God, N., is baptized into the name of the Father, and of the Son, and of the Holy Spirit, now and for ever, even unto ages of ages,

Amen,' sinking and raising him at the utterance of each name." [194]

The ritual of the Greek Church in Russia is as follows:

"The priest baptizes him, holding him upright and turning his face toward the East, saying, 'N., the servant of God, is baptized in the name of the Father. Amen.' (First immersion.) 'In the name of the Son. Amen.' (Second immersion.) 'In the name of the Holy Spirit. Amen.' (Third immersion.) 'Now and for ever, even unto ages of ages. Amen.'"

The language of the Larger Catechism of the Græco-Russian Church we have given on pages 191, 192. The Shorter Catechism answers the question, "In what consists baptism?" as follows:

"In this, that the believer is dipped thrice in water, in the name of the Father, and of the Son, and of the Holy Spirit."

The ritual of the Roman Catholic Church is as follows:

"Then the godfather or godmother, or both, holding the infant, the priest takes the baptismal water in a little vessel or jug, and pours the same three times upon the head of the infant, in the form of the cross, and at the same time he says, uttering the words once only, distinctly and attentively, 'N., I baptize thee in the name of the Fa+ther' (he pours the first time), 'and of the + Son' (he pours a second time), 'and of the Holy + Ghost' (he pours a third time)."

The Shorter Catechism describes the act of baptism as follows:

"Water is poured upon the head of the person to be baptized, while these words are pronounced: 'I baptize thee in the name of the Father, and of the Son, and of the Holy Ghost. Amen.' The water must be common and natural water, and must be poured on by the same person who repeats the words; and care must be taken to repeat the words exactly, and to pronounce them at the same time that the water is poured on."

The Rubric of the Church of England reads as follows:

"And then, naming it [the child] after them (if they shall certify him that the child may well endure it), he shall dip it in the water discreetly and warily, saying, 'N., I baptize thee,' etc.

"But if they shall certify that the child is weak, it shall suffice to pour water upon it."

The Rubric of the Protestant Episcopal Church in the United States is as follows:

"And then, naming it after them, he shall dip it

in the water discreetly, or shall pour water upon it, saying, ' N., I baptize thee,' " etc.

The following is the order for the baptism of infants in the Methodist Episcopal Church:

" Then the minister shall take the child into his hands, and say to the friends of the child, ' Name this child.' And then, naming it after them, he shall sprinkle or pour water upon it, or, if desired, immerse it in water, saying, ' N., I baptize thee,' " etc.

The order for the baptism of adults reads thus:

" Then shall the minister ask the name of each person to be baptized; and shall sprinkle or pour water upon him (or, if he shall desire it, shall immerse him in water), saying, ' N., I baptize thee,' " etc.

The Presbyterian Confession of Faith has the following in reference to baptism:

" The outward element to be used in this sacrament is water, wherewith the party is to be baptized in the name of the Father, and of the Son, and of the Holy Ghost, by a minister of the gospel, lawfully called thereunto.

" Dipping of the person into the water is not necessary; but baptism is rightly administered by pouring or sprinkling water upon the person."

The " Directions for Baptism " are as follows:

THE ACT OF BAPTISM. 203

"Then the minister is to pray for a blessing to attend this ordinance; after which, calling the child by its name, he shall say, 'I baptize thee in the name of the Father, and of the Son, and of the Holy Ghost.'

"As he pronounces these words he is to baptize the child with water by pouring or sprinkling it on the face of the child, without adding any other ceremony; and the whole shall be concluded with prayer."

The American Dutch Reformed Church makes this declaration:

"*First.* That we, with our children, are conceived and born in sin, and therefore are children of wrath, insomuch that we cannot enter into the kingdom of God, except we are born again. This, the dipping in or sprinkling with water, teaches us, whereby the impurity of our souls is signified, and we admonished to loathe and humble ourselves before God, and seek for our purification and salvation without ourselves.

"*Secondly.* Holy baptism witnesseth and sealeth unto us the washing away of our sins through Jesus Christ. Therefore we are baptized in the name of the Father, and of the Son, and of the Holy Ghost."

Baptist, Congregationalist, Freewill-Baptist, and

many other churches, have no authoritative order of baptism.

REMARKS.

During this period, in the Roman Catholic Church, the prevailing practice has been pouring. And this is the teaching of the Roman rituals now in use. Immersion, however, is recognized in the ritual of the Bishop of Quebec, in 1703, and in the Bamberg *Instructional* of 1773. It is also still practised in the cathedral at Milan; although, according to Rev. Hugh Jones, D. D., President of Llangollen College, Wales, who was at Milan in 1877, the immersion is not entire. In a communication to the London *Baptist*, written shortly after his visit, he says: "I went to the cathedral and made inquiries of one of the officials of the church respecting the manner of baptizing there; he, not understanding what I said, brought to me an Italian gentleman knowing the English language. I repeated my question to him. He replied, that in that church they follow the Ambrosian ritual, and that they immerse the child. 'Do they completely immerse the whole body?' I added. 'No,' he continued, 'but the back part of the head, including the ears and the forehead.' 'So the ceremony of complete immersion is no longer observed?' I said again; and he replied, 'No.' Thinking that it was possible that this man was misleading me (he appeared, however, to be a man of culture and well informed), I went to another person, who was selling a

Description of the Cathedral of Milan, receiving the fees for ascending the roof, etc., and asked him the very same questions which I had put to the other gentleman; his answer was exactly the same, almost word for word." If this testimony correctly represents the present practice in the administration of baptism in the Milan cathedral, there has been a recent encroachment upon the ancient ritual which bears the name of Ambrose.

In the Greek Church immersion has held its place in the administration of baptism as in the preceding centuries. Not long after his accession to the pontificate, the late Pope Pius IX. addressed a letter to the Christians of the East, inviting them to return to the Roman Church. The Patriarch of Constantinople called together the Patriarchs of Alexandria, Antioch, and Jerusalem, and about thirty archbishops and bishops, to consider this "papal aggression." An encyclical letter, embodying the results of their deliberations, was published in Corfu, in 1848, soon after the synod adjourned. In this document the practice of the Roman Church in baptism is characterized as an innovation— a departure from the apostolic form, a substitution of sprinkling instead of baptism, and as making superfluous the baptism which the Lord delivered to the church. In harmony with the testimony of De Stourdza and of the ritual of the Greek Church is the testimony of Rev. A. N. Arnold, D. D., formerly missionary of the American Baptist Missionary Union to Greece. In an article on "Baptism in the Greek

Church," in the *Baptist Quarterly* for January, 1870, he says: "The writer has repeatedly seen baptism administered according to the Greek ritual, and in every instance it has been a triple immersion. If, as may sometimes happen, any little portion of the body is not completely submerged when the child is placed naked in the font, the priest, by a movement of his hand, sends a wave over it. The only instance of adult baptism that came within his knowledge was that of a converted Jew; and in his case, the ordinary fonts, of course, being too small for the purpose, a tub or tank was constructed for the occasion, and placed in the church. In the course of more than eleven years' residence and missionary service among the Greeks, he never heard the slightest intimation of any diversity of views or laxity of practice among them on the subject of baptism, except on this one point: the National Greek Church of Russia has for the last two centuries consented to receive converts from the Romish Church and Trinitarian Protestants without rebaptism." The other sections of the Greek Church do not.

Some travellers have asserted that baptism is performed in the Greek Church by sprinkling, and they have witnessed such an administration of the ordinance. It should be added, therefore, that a service of ablution has a place in the Greek baptismal ritual, only it is performed seven days after the baptism. The ritual reads as follows: "After seven days the child is again brought to the church for the ablu-

THE ACT OF BAPTISM. 207

tion. After three short prayers, the priest loosens the child's girdle and garment, and uniting the ends of them wets them with clean water and sprinkles [ῥαίνει] the child, saying, 'Thou hast been justified, thou hast been enlightened.'" It is evidently this service which these travellers have mistaken for baptism.

A few years ago there was an effort to bring together the Greek Church and the Church of England. In a pamphlet published by the Russo-Greek committee, there is an abstract of a conference between the Archbishop of Syra, representing the Greek Church, and the Bishop of Ely and others, representing the Church of England. Concerning baptism, there is this record in the pamphlet:

"ARCHBISHOP.—As to the form of baptism. Threefold immersion was the custom of the early church. Rom. vi. 4 is only thus explicable.

"BISHOP.—Immersion was the original custom; but possibly on account of the climate, the northern nations have exchanged it for affusion. This is the case in parts of the Eastern Church, as North Russia, Servia, and Montenegro. The *rule* in the Rubric of the Church of England is that of immersion.

"ARCHBISHOP.—If affusion is used in Servia, it is an abuse. I found the same in several instances in Syra, and at once corrected it.

"BISHOP.—We allow that immersion is the most ancient and the most correct form, but we do not regard the present form as invalid. The form by immersion is better than the form by affusion. It would be well if it could be restored."

The Armenian Church a century ago, in the baptismal service, united immersion and aspersion. At what time this custom had its origin we are unable to learn. According to an unpublished translation of the Armenian ritual by Rev. S. C. Malan, quoted in the article on "Baptism" in Smith's *Dictionary of Christian Antiquities* (p. 169), the priest first lets the child or catechumen down into the water and buries him therein three times, as a figure of Christ's three days' burial. Then, taking the child out of the water, he thrice pours a handful of water on his head. This is also the testimony of Rev. H. G. O. Dwight, as given on page 196. It will be seen that this ritual differs from that given by Assemanus, in that the affusion follows the immersion.

In the ritual of the Church of England immersion has been recognized throughout this period, though the ancient practice has been almost wholly displaced. Many have regretted this displacement, and have labored earnestly "for the retrieving of the use of it according to the Rubric of the church;" but they have labored in vain. Baptism by immersion, however, occasionally takes place in the Church of England. In an English journal we read that "on Sunday, December 2, 1877, at Christ Church, Wellington, Shropshire, the Rev. Mr. Butler, the vicar, at the morning service baptized by immersion, in a large bath provided for the occasion, the daughter, aged eight years, of Dr. Cranage, Principal of the celebrated Old Hall School for boys in that town." A recent London paper has this paragraph: "A Bacup local journal, in reporting the anniversary of the St. Saviour's Church schools, remarks, 'In the morning Rev. E. Thring baptized by immersion a young man from Smithy Bridge. The rite was performed in the baptistery provided for those churchmen who may conscientiously desire baptism in this mode of its administration. Unlike the fonts at many churches, that at St. Saviour's Church is suitable for both sprinkling and immersion; but this is only the second baptism of the kind that has been performed in that church that we remember."

In the Protestant Episcopal Church in the United States, also, there have been those who have expressed a desire to return to the ancient rite of immersion. It should be noticed that the American Rubric omits the words of the English Rubric, "But if they certify that the child is weak, it shall suffice to pour water upon it." Unlike the English Rubric, therefore, it does not require the immersion of healthy infants.

In the Presbyterian Church, in the early part of this period, according to the testimony of Baxter, pouring only was practised. The directions for baptism now in use in the Presbyterian churches in the United States specify "pouring or sprinkling;" but the former has given place to the latter.

The present attitude of the Presbyterian denomination in reference to the act of baptism may be inferred from the fact that, in 1876, Rev. J. H. Clark of the Lackawanna Presbytery, in Pennsylvania, immersed an applicant for membership in the church of which he was pastor. His presbytery having censured the act, he appealed to the Synod of Philadelphia, which after a review of the case, by a majority of one, accepted the following: "In view of the teachings and principles entering into the doctrine of baptism, we judge that the administration of baptism by Rev. J. H. Clark in the case excepted to came within the possible limits of a permissible administration of the rite, and although without any sanction of command or fact in sacred Scriptures, yet did not involve a moral wrong. The mode of administration, however, not being accordant with the distinctive mode of baptism accepted and appointed by the Presbyterian Church, **we do approve of the spirit of the exception of the Presbytery of Lackawanna, as** betokening a just, watchful care in the exercise of its responsible duties, and **adjudge** that it should be so interpreted as giving fraternal counsel, and not as ecclesiastical censure."

In an editorial in the *Presbyterian* of October 28, 1876, a paper published in Philadelphia, occurred the following in a reference to this case: "One thing is evident to us, and that is that a change of opinion is gradually taking place on this subject. The number of men in the Presbyterian ministry who believe that immersion is not baptism is increasing."

Such men there have been among the Congregationalists—at least, a book entitled *Immersion not Baptism* was written and published a few years ago by a Congregationalist minister. It should be said, however, that while sprinkling has been the rule in the administration of baptism in Congregational churches in this country from the time of the Pilgrims, there has been during the past twenty-five years an increasing willingness on the part of many Congregational pastors to immerse candidates for baptism who look upon immersion as the scriptural act.

In the Methodist Episcopal Church in the United States, sprinkling or immersion is practised in administering the rite of baptism, according to the preference of the candidate. Those who prefer sprinkling are the larger number, while the number of those who prefer immersion is constantly growing smaller.

The Freewill-Baptists in the United States have insisted on immersion as the only scriptural baptism. At their General Conference, held in Providence, R. I., in 1874, however, it was voted to receive to membership persons who, in uniting with other churches, had been sprinkled. But this action was revoked, without discussion, at the General Conference held at Fairport, N. Y., in 1877.

It should be added that there are Baptist churches in England in which unimmersed members of other evangelical churches are received to membership. But in Baptist churches in the United States this is never done. The members of these churches hold, as their predecessors have held in all the history of the denomination in this country, that immersion only, into the name of the Father, and of the Son, and of the Holy Spirit, is valid baptism, and that sprinkling is a substitute for which there is no warrant in the Scripture records.

GENERAL REVIEW.

The testimony now presented in reference to the act of baptism in the history of the church warrants the following statements:

1. In the New Testament period baptism was administered by immersion, and by immersion only.

2. In the third century, in Cyprian's letter to Magnus, we read for the first time of pouring as a substitute for immersion. It was practised, however, in cases of necessity only, as when death was thought to be impending and the person was unbaptized. It was not claimed that such an administration of the rite had New Testament authority.

3. Tertullian is the first witness to trine immersion —a practice which had its origin evidently in the discussions in reference to the Trinity, and which was soon generally recognized in the Christian Church, only the Eunomians practising single immersion until the seventh century, when Gregory the Great, and afterward, in 633, the Fourth Council of Toledo, sanctioned single immersion in Spain.

4. In other parts of Christendom trine immersion held its place in the seventh and eighth centuries. In the ninth century, in order to prevent a schism,

THE ACT OF BAPTISM. 213

the Council of Worms reaffirmed the decision of the Fourth Toledo Council. With this exception, and the exception of the cases of supposed necessity, baptism, until the thirteenth century, was generally trine immersion.

5. Thomas Aquinas, who died near the close of the thirteenth century, was the first, so far as we can learn, to justify sprinkling or pouring as New Testament baptism.

6. At the beginning of the fourteenth century adult baptism had given place almost wholly to infant baptism; and in some localities, at this time, pouring had become so common that at the Council of Ravenna, in 1311, pouring and immersion were declared to be equally valid.

7. In the Greek Church, and in many places in the Roman Church, the ancient practice of immersion was still retained. In England, at the opening of the sixteenth century, immersion was the rule; while in Germany, except in the northern part, sprinkling or pouring had superseded the earlier form.

8. In 1525, on the part of some of the Anabaptists of Switzerland, there was a return to immersion, and the older Protestant liturgies gave the preference to the primitive form. But Calvin threw the weight of his influence in favor of sprinkling, and the English and Scotch exiles, who had adopted the practice of the Genevan Church, introduced the change on their return from the Continent, and immersion gradually disappeared. In the Westminster Assembly, in 1644,

by a very close vote, all reference to immersion was omitted in the Directory for Public Worship. Since then, in the Presbyterian Church, sprinkling has been the rule, to which, at the present time, there is hardly an exception.

9. Since the sixteenth century, in the Church of England, immersion has been less and less observed, though the ritual has remained unchanged and still requires the ancient form, unless it shall be certified that the child is weak. But in the Church of England and in the Protestant Episcopal Church in this country, earnest desire has been expressed by some for a return to immersion.

10. In the Greek Church there has been no change in the form of baptism, and trine immersion is still required. In the Roman Church, after the fourteenth century, pouring more and more became the rule, and now knows no exception, except at Milan.

11. In the Armenian Church, during the past century, immersion and pouring have been united in the administration of baptism.

12. The appearance of the Baptists in England in the seventeenth century was a protest against the change from immersion to sprinkling. In this they have been followed by several minor religious bodies, while in some others there is an increased willingness to practise immersion. In the Methodist Episcopal Church, however, in which both sprinkling and immersion are allowed, the latter is more and more giving place to the former.

NOTES.

[1] SEE also Schneckenburger, *Ueber das Alter der jüd. Proselytentaufe*, Berlin, 1828, and especially an article by Prof. C. H. Toy in *The Baptist Quarterly* for July, 1872.

[2] In their first London edition, Liddell & Scott gave the following definition of *baptizein:* I. *To dip repeatedly, dip under, to bathe, to steep, wet, to pour upon, drench.* II. *To dip a vessel, to draw water.* III. To baptize. The first American edition followed literally the first English edition. In the second English edition, instead of *to dip under*, we find *to sink*, referring to ships; while *to steep, wet, pour upon, drench*, are omitted. The second American edition conformed to the second English edition, and in none of the subsequent editions have these words reappeared.

[3] Βαπτίζω, f. σῶ, *to dip in* or *under water.* Aristoph. Φίλων 1; of ships, *to sink* them. Polyb. 2, 51, 6, etc.: ἐβάπτισαν τὴν πόλιν, metaph. of the crowds who flocked into Jerusalem at the time of the siege, Joseph. B. J. 4, 3, 3. Pass. ὡς ἐκ τοῦ βεβαπτίσθαι ἀνὰ πνέουσι. Hippocr. 5, 242 (Litré): *to bathe.* Eubul. Ναυσικ. I. metaph., βεβαπτισμένοι, *soaked in wine;* Lat., *vino madidi*, Plut. Symp. 176 B; ὀφλήμασι βεβ., *over head and ears* in debt, Plut. Galb. 21; γνοὺς βαπτιζόμενον τὸ μειράκιον, seeing him *drowned* with questions, Heind. Plat. Enthyd. 177 D. II. Φιάλαις β. ἐκ . . . κρατήρων, *to draw wine from bowls in cups* (of course *by dipping* them), Plut. Alex. 67; cf. βάπτω, I. 3. III. *To baptize*, N. T., Eccl. Liddell & Scott's *Greek-English Lexicon, sixth English ed., 1875.*

[4] Βαπτίζω, f. ίσω, aor. 1 ἐβάπτισα, ptcp. pf. pass. βεβαπτισμένος, aor. 1 pass. ἐβαπτίσθην, fut. 1 pass. βαπτιθήσομαι, aor. 1 mid. ἐβαπτισάμην (frequentative from βάπτω, as βαλλίζω from βάλλω); so in Plat., Polyb., Diod., Strab., Joseph., Plut., and others. I. (1.) *To immerse repeatedly, to immerse, to submerge* (of sunken ships, Pol. 1, 51, 6; 8, 8, 4; of animals, Diod. 1, 36). (2.) *To bathe, lave, cleanse with water by immersion or*

submersion; mid. and aor. 1 pass. *to lave myself;* so Mark vii. 4, Luke xi. 38; (2 Kings v. 14: ἐβαπτίσατο ἐν τῷ 'Ιορδάνῃ = טָבַל; Lev. xxxiv. 27; Judith xii. 8). (3.) *To overwhelm, as* ἰδιώτας ταῖς εἰσφοραῖς, Diod. 1, 73; ὀφλήμασι, Plut. Galba 21; τῇ συμφορᾷ βεβαπτισμένος, Heliod. Æth. 2, 3; and simply to inflict on one severe and great abundant calamities; ἐβάπτισαν τὴν πόλιν, Jos. B. Jud. 4, 3,3; ἡ ἀνομία με βαπτίσει, LXX. Jes. 21, 4; hence βαπτίζεσθαι βάπτισμα (comp. Win, p. 201; comp. λούεσθαι τὸ λουτρόν, Æl. H. A. 3, 42); *to be submerged with calamities*, of those upon whom they are inflicted to be borne, Matt. xx. 22 f., Mark x. 38 f., Luke xii. 50 (comp. the German phrase *etwas auszubaden haben*, and phrases which are properly used of those who wade through rivers of water: ἕως τῶν πάντων οἱ πεζοὶ βαπτιζόμενοι διέβαινον, Pol. 3, 72, 4). II. In the New Testament it is used especially of the solemn rite of holy bathing, first instituted by John the Baptist, afterward received by Christians as a command of Christ, and accommodated to the genius and nature of his religion (see under βάπτισμα)—that is, immersion in water, so performed that it might be a sign of sins and guilt washed away, received by those who, influenced by a desire for salvation, wished to be admitted to the benefits of the Messianic kingdom. (*a*) Absolutely, *to administer the rite of holy bathing, to baptize;* Vulgate, *tingo, tingus* (Tertull.); Mark i. 4; John i. 25, 28; iii. 22 f., 26; iv. 2; x. 40; 1 Cor. i. 17; with corresponding noun τὸ βάπτισμα, Acts xix. 4; ὁ βαπτίζων, substantive ὁ βαπτιστής, Mark vi. 14; τινά, John iv. 1; Acts viii. 38; 1 Cor. i. 14, 16. Pass., *to be baptized*, Matt. iii. 13 f., 16; Mark xvi. 16; Luke iii. 21; Acts ii. 41; viii. 12, 13; x. 47; xvi. 15; 1 Cor. i. 15 (Lachm. Tischdf.); x. 2 (Lachm.). Pass. in a reflexive sense, *to desire to be baptized, to receive baptism*, Luke vii. 30; Acts ii. 38; ix. 18; xvi. 33: xviii. 8; xxii. 16; also corresponding noun τὸ βάπτισμα, Luke vii. 29; 1 aor. mid., 1 Cor. x. 2 (Lachm. ἐβαπτίσθησαν); Acts xxii. 16; followed by the dative of the substance in which the immersion is performed, ὕδατι, see below. (*b*) With prepositions. (*aa*) εἰς, denoting the *material* into which one is immersed: εἰς τὸν 'Ιορδάνην, Mark i. 9. Denoting the *end*: εἰς μετάνοιαν, that one is pledged to amendment of character, Matt. iii. 11; εἰς τὸ 'Ιωάννου βάπτισμα, that he is pledged to duties which are imposed by the baptism of John, Acts xix. 3; εἰς ὄνομά τινος, professing the name (see under ὄνομα) of some one whom we follow as a leader, Matt. xxviii. 19; Acts viii. 16; xix. 5; 1 Cor. i. 13, 15; εἰς ἄφεσιν ἁμαρτιῶν, seeking the remission of sins, Acts ii.

38; εἰς τὸν Μωϋσῆν, that they should follow Moses as a leader, 1 Cor. x. 2. Denoting the *effect:* εἰς ἐν σῶμα, by baptism to bind together into one body, 1 Cor. xii. 13; εἰς Χριστόν, εἰς τόν θάνατον αὐτοῦ, by baptism to bring about union with Christ, union with death encountered by him, in which union we became dead to sin, Gal. iii. 27; Rom. vi. 5. (*bb*) ἐν, with the dative of the substance into which one is immersed, ἐν τῷ 'Ιορδάνῃ, Mark i. 5; ἐν τῷ ὕδατι, John i. 31 (Lachm. ἐν ὑδ.; but compare Meyer); of that with which any one baptizes: ἐν ὕδατι, Matt. iii. 11; Mark i. 8; John i. 25, 31 (Lachm.), 33; comp. Bttm. ntl. Gr., p. 158, 10; with simple dative, ὕδατι, Luke iii. 16; xi. 16; Acts i. 5; ἐν πνεύματι, to imbue largely with the Holy Spirit (according to the same figure by which his abundant bestowment is called a *pouring out*), Matt. iii. 11; Mark i. 8; Luke iii. 16; John i. 33; Acts i. 5; xi. 16; also καὶ πυρί (those who do not receive him), to overwhelm with fire—that is, to punish with the severest torments of hell, Matt. iii. 11; ἐν ὀνόματι τοῦ κυρίου, with the authority of the Lord, Acts x. 48. (*cc*) Pass. ἐπὶ τῷ ὀνόματι 'Ιησοῦ Χριστοῦ, trusting in the name of Jesus Christ—that is, so that he rests his hope in him, Acts ii. 38. (*dd*) ὑπέρ τῶν νεκρῶν, for the dead—that is, for giving eternal salvation to them, so that we submit to baptism in their place, 1 Cor. xv. 29; compare especially Neander on this passage, Rückert Progr. concerning this passage Jen., 1847; *Paret.* in Ewald, Jahrb. d. Bibl. Wissenschaft., ix. p. 247.

Βάπτισμα, *immersion, submersion*—1. trop. of calamities and afflictions by which one is overwhelmed on all sides. . . . 2. Of *John's baptism*, that rite of purification by which men, having confessed their sins, were bound to a reformation of character, obtained the remission of their sins previously committed, and would soon become worthy of the benefits of the coming Messianic kingdom. . . . 3. Of *Christian baptism*: according to the apostolic conception, this is the rite of holy submersion commanded by Christ, by which men, having confessed their sins and professed the faith which they have in Christ, are regenerated by the Holy Spirit to a new life, come into the fellowship of Christ and the church, 1 Cor. xii. 13, and are made partakers of eternal salvation, Eph. iv. 5. C. L. W. Grimm's edition of Wilke's *New Testament Greek*, 1868.

⁵ Βαπτίζω, ίσω; (βάπτω), *to dip, to immerse; to sink.* Pindar's ἀβάπτιστος shows the antiquity of this verb. *Aristopon* (Comic). Philomid. Pseud-*Alcib.* (Bergk, p. 473), -ινὰ κύ-

πασι πόντου. *Heron* 192, -σθαι εἰς τὸ ὕδωρ. *Polyb.* 1, 51, 6; 3, 72, 4; 5, 47, 2; 8, 8, 4; 16, 6, 2. *Diod.* 16, 80. *Strab.* 6, 2, 9; 12, 2, 4; 14, 3, 9. *Jos.* Ant. 4, 4, 6, τῆς τέφρας ταύτης εἰς τὴν πηγήν; 9, 10, 2, -σθαι; 15, 3, 3. B. J. 3, 8, 5; 1, 22, 2, -σθαι ἐν τῇ κολυμβήθρᾳ; 2, 20, 1. Vit. 3. *Hermes Tr.*, Poem 35, 16, τινὰ εἴς τι; 36, 4 Ἐβαπτίσαντο τοῦ νοός, in mind. *Epict.* Frag. 14 -σθαι, to be drowned, as the effect of sinking. *Plut.* I. 731, D; 702, C Φιάλαις . . . ἐκ πίθων μεγάλων, by dipping them. II. 820, C 914, D, τὸν Διόνυσον πρὸς τὴν θάλασσαν; 166, A, τινὰ εἴς τι; 971, B, τὰ ἀγγεῖα; 990, D, ἑαυτὸν εἰς τὴν Κωπαΐδα λίμνην. *Lucian.* I. 157; II. 107. *Poll.* 1, 114; 124 *Clem. A.* II. 640, C -σθαι, to sink. *Dion.* C. 37, 58, 3. *Joann. Mosch.* 2900, A -σθαι ἕως τραχήλου. Tropically: *Eubul.* (Comic.), Nausic, to afflict. *Euenus* 2, 5, p. 474 (Bergk.) *Plut.* Euth. 277, D; Conv. 176, B, βεβαπτισμένος; L. *madidus*, soaked in liquor, intoxicated. *Sept.* Esai. 21, 4. *Diod.* 1, 73. *Philon.* 1, 91, 10; 224, 30, συμφοραῖς τὴν ψυχήν; II. 478, 25 -σθαι, to be drunk; 647, 5. *Jos.* Ant. 10, 9, 4. B. J. 4, 3, 3, τὴν πόλιν, like a ship. *Plut.* II. 9, B; 593, F; 656, D; 975, C -ισμένος, intoxicated; I. 1062, C Πεντακισχιλίων μυριάδων ὀφλήμασι βεβαπτισμένον, œre alieno oppressum. *Just.* Tryph. 86, p. 681, C Βεβαπτισμένους ταῖς βαρυτάταις ἁμαρτίαις. *Lucian.* III. 81. *Sibyll.* 5, 478, of the setting sun. *Aquil.*, Job ix. 31, ἐν διαφθορᾷ. *Clem. A.* 1, 57, A Ἀγνοίᾳ βεβαπτισμένος, sunk in ignorance; 421, A -σθαι εἰς ὕπνον. *Plotin.* I. 70, 1, Βαπτισθεὶς ἢ νόσοις, ἢ μάγων τέχναις; 155, ἐν τῷ σώματι. *Basil.* IV. 996, D. *Theod.* III. 1148, A.

2. Mid. βαπτίζομαι, to perform ablution, to bathe. *Sept.* Reg. 4, 5, 13; Judith xii. 7; Sie. 31, 30 -σθαι ἀπὸ νεκροῦ (Lev. xi. 25, seq.; Num. xix. 18, seq.). *Marc.* 7, 4. *Luc.* 11, 38. *Just.* Tryph. 46. *Clem. A.* I. 1184, B; 1352, C (Lev. xv. 18); II. 649, C -σθαι τοῖς δάκρυσι, bathed in tears.

3. *To plunge* a knife. *Jos.* B. J. 2, 18, 4, Εἰς τὴν ἑαυτοῦ σφαγὴν ἐβάπτισε τὸ ξίφος. *Galen.* X. 150, E, F, of surgical instruments. Pseudo-*Plut.* Vit. Hom. 1091, B.

4. Baptizo, mergo, mergito, tingo or tinguo, to baptize. *N. T.* passim. *Ignat.* 713, B. *Just.* Tryph. 29. *Tertull.* I. 1207, A; 1812, A, B; 1214, A; II. 964, A. *Theod.* Her, 1368, A. *Basil.* IV. 129, B. *Const. Apost.* 7, 25; 8, 37, ὁ βαπτιζόμενος, candidate for baptism. *Can. Apost.* 47, ἄνωθεν = ἀναβαπτίζειν. *Theod.* IV. 420, B. [*Porph.* Adm. 149, 9, βαπτισμένος = βεβαπτισμένος. There is no evidence that Luke and Paul and the other writers of the New Testament put upon this verb meanings not recognized by the Greeks.] E. A. Sophocles'

NOTES. 219

Greek Lexicon of the Roman and Byzantine Periods, Boston, 1870.

⁶ His definition is very full: Βαπτίζω, aor. 1 Pass. ἐβαπτίσθην; aor. 1 mid. ἐβαπτισάμην, only in Acts xxii. 16; 1 Cor. x. 2; *immerse, submerge;* often in later Gk. Plut. de superst. 166, A, βάπτισον σεαυτὸν εἰς θάλασσαν; LXX. once = טָבַל, 2 Kings v. 14: ἐβαπτίσατο ἐν τῷ Ἰορδάνῃ. Metaphor., *e. g.* Plut. Galb. 21: ὀφλήμασι βεβαπτισμένος; cf. Isa. xxi. 4: ἡ ἀνομία με βαπτίζει = בָּעָה.

The peculiar New Testament and Christian use for the designation of *immersion, submersion* for a religious purpose = baptize, John i. 25: τί οὖν βαπτίζεις, may be safely traced back to the Levitical washings, Hebr. רחץ, Lev. xiv. 8, 9; xv. 5, 6, 7, 8, 10, 11, 16, 18, 21, 22, 27; xvii. 15; xv. 13; xvi. 4, 24, 26, 28; Num. xix. 7, 19; Ex. xix. 10; xxix. 4; xl. 12, for which LXX. = λούεσθαι; cf. Acts xxii. 16: βάπτισαι καὶ ἀπόλουσαι τὰς ἁμαρτίας σου. For according to Mark vii. 4; Luke xi. 38; Heb. ix. 10; Ecclus. 34, 10: βαπτιζόμενος ἀπὸ νεκροῦ, βαπτίζειν appears to have been at that time the technical term for these washings; cf. Matt. xv. 2: νίπτεσθαι, for which Mark vii. 4 has βαπτίζεσθαι. (Out of these washings certainly arose the baptism of proselytes, which, according to the testimonies as to its age, cannot have suggested the New Testament βαπτίζειν. Vid. Schneckenburger, *Ueber das Alter der jüdischen Proselytentaufe*, 1828; Winer, *Realwört s. v. Proselyten:* "Josephus, Philo, and the older Targumists never allude to the baptism of proselytes, properly so termed—a baptism which was deemed as essential as circumcision—although they had frequent opportunities of doing so."—Leyrer in Herzog's *Realencyclopœdie*, 12, 242 ff.) As the terms טבל, טבילה were used in post-biblical Hebrew, rather than the Biblical word רחץ, to denote these washings, and the former had already been rendered βάπτεις by the LXX. (vid. supra), it is intelligible enough how this use arose. Cf. 2 Kings v. 10, where, v. 14, βαπτίζειν. Expressions like Isa. i. 16, and prophecies like Ezra xxxvi. 25; xxxvii. 23 ff.; Zech. xiii. 1 were suggested by the Levitical washings. These washings again and the prophecies in question are connected with the purification which followed on and completed the act of expiation or cleansing from sin; cf. s. v. καθαρίζω, καθαρισμός; cf. Num. viii. 5-22; Lev. xiii. 14; Ex. xix. 14; also 1 John v. 6: οὗτός ἐστιν ὁ ἐλθὼν δι' ὕδατος καὶ αἵματος, κ.τ.λ.; Heb. x 22, 23: ῥεραντισμένοι τὰς καρδίας ἀπὸ συνειδήσεως πονηρᾶς καὶ λελουμένοι τὸ σῶμα ὕδατι καθαρῷ. This is the reason also why βαπτίζειν in itself was not a thing unknown to the Jews, and why they did not consider it right for every one to come forward as John the Baptist did, John i. 25. For what was unusual in John was that he performed the βαπτίζειν on others, whereas the law required such lustrations to be accomplished by every one for himself. His was an act which only had a parallel in Lev. viii. 6, and could not but call to mind the prophecies in question; and indeed the Rabbis testify (vid. Lightfoot, Horæ Hebr. in John i. 25) that corresponding expectations were entertained, *e. g.*, concerning the future of Elias. Kimchi, on Zech. ix. 6, says: "tradunt Rabbini: Elias purificabit nothos eosque restituet congregationi."

By βαπτίζειν, therefore, we must understand *a washing* which, like that of the theocratic washings and purifications, is designed *to purge away sin*. Cf. John iii. 25 ff., where both the baptism of Jesus and that of John are included under the idea of καθαρισμός. Hence Matt. iii. 6: ἐβαπτίζοντο—ἐξομολογούμενοι τὰς ἁμαρτίας αὐτῶν; Mark i. 4: ἐγένετο Ἰωάννης ὁ βαπτίζων ἐν τῇ ἐρήμῳ κηρύσσων βάπτισμα μετανοίας εἰς ἄφεσιν ἁμαρτιῶν. Cf. Luke iii. 3; Acts ii. 38: βαπτισθήτω ἕκαστος ὑμῶν—εἰς ἄφεσιν ἁμαρτιῶν; Acts xxii. 16: βάπτισαι καὶ ἀπόλουσαι τὰς ἁμαρτίας σου; 1 Pet. iii. 21, vid. s. v. βάπτισμα. So far, therefore, there is no difference between the baptism of John and Christian baptism, as both aim at the ἄφεσις ἁμ. The expression βαπτίζω ὑμᾶς ἐν ὕδατι εἰς μετάνοιαν, Matt. iii. 11, means nothing more than Mark i. 4: βάπτισμα μετανοίας εἰς ἄφεσιν ἁμαρτιῶν, and Acts ii. 38: Μετανοήσατε καὶ βαπτισθήτω, κ.τ.λ., vid. supra. Not as though μετάνοια were to be worked by this baptism in the place of ἄφεσις, but ἄφεσις cannot be without μετάνοια; without which also no one can enter the kingdom of heaven; it is required too of all who come to baptism, Matt. iii. 2; viii.; Acts ii. 38; it remains accordingly the distinctive characteristic of those who are baptized for the remission of sins. To bring about such μετάνοια, John appeared βαπτίζων ἐν ὕδατι; and the expression in Matt. iii. 11 is selected instead of εἰς ἄφεσιν ἁμ. in view vs. 7, 8. The expression implies notwithstanding that there is a distinction between the baptism of John and that of the Messianic church, in which μετάνοια is appropriated by πίστις. The baptism of John is styled κατ'. ἐξ., the βάπτισμα μετανοίας in Mark i. 4; Luke iii. 3; Acts xiii. 24; xix. 4; we might accordingly designate Christian baptism βάπτισμα πίστεως, coll. Acts xix. 4, 5: Ἰωάννης μὲν ἐβάπτισεν βάπτισμα μετανοίας, τῷ λαῷ λέγων εἰς τὸν ἐρχόμενον μετ' αὐτὸν ἵνα πιστεύσωσιν, τοῦτ' ἐστιν εἰς τὸν Ἰν. ἀκούσαντες δὲ ἐβαπτίσθησαν εἰς τὸ ὄνομα τοῦ κυρίου Ἰυ., Acts viii. 12, 13. The difference lies, however, not in the βαπτίζειν, which was in all cases a washing unto purification from sin, but in the temporal relation thereof to Jesus Christ. For all depends on what is had in view at the immersion or washing; Acts xix. 3: εἰς τί οὖν ἐβαπτίσθητε; οἱ δὲ εἶπαν· εἰς τὸ Ἰωάννον βάπτισμα; v. 5: ἐβαπτίσθησαν εἰς τὸ ὄνομα τοῦ κυρίου Ἰυ.; 1 Cor. i. 13: ἦ εἰς τὸ ὄνομα Παύλου ἐβαπτίσθητε; v. 15: ἵνα μή τις εἴπῃ ὅτι εἰς τὸ ἐμὸν ὄνομα ἐβαπτίσθητε; x. 2: πάνπες εἰς τὸν Μωϋσῆν ἐβαπτίσαντο, on which cf. Ex. xiv. 31: וַיַּאֲמִינוּ בַּיהוָה וּבְמֹשֶׁה עַבְדּוֹ. What is in question is a relation into which the candidates for baptism are to be brought; as also in the case of εἰς μετάνοιαν, εἰς ἄφεσιν ἁμαρτιῶν, εἰς ἓν σῶμα ἐβαπτίσθημεν, 1 Cor. xii. 13—expressions which differ from those previously mentioned only as the relation to a person differs from that to a thing. Εἰς is invariably used in an ideal sense. That the local force of the preposition must not be pressed as though it ought to be explained in analogy with Mark i. 9—ἐβαπτίσθη ὑπὸ Ἰωάννου εἰς τὸν Ἰορδάνην—is plain from the expressions last adduced, especially from 1 Cor. x. 2: πάντες εἰς τὸν Μωϋσῆν ἐβαπτίσαντο ἐν τῇ νεφέλῃ καὶ ἐν τῇ θαλάσσῃ; Matt. iii. 11: ἐν ὕδατι εἰς μετάνοιαν. A complete explanation is thus furnished of Rom. vi. 3, 4: ὅσοι ἐβαπτίσθημεν εἰς Χν Ἰν, εἰς τὸν φάνατον αὐτοῦ ἐβαπτίσθημεν· συνετάφημεν οὖν αὐτῷ διὰ τοῦ βαπτίσματος εἰς τὸν θάνατον. Further conjoined with εἰς in Matt. xxviii. 19: εἰς τὸ ὄνομα τοῦ πατρὸς καὶ τοῦ υἱοῦ καὶ τοῦ ἁγίου πνεύματος; Gal. iii. 37: ὅσοι εἰς Χν ἐβαπτίσθητε, Χν ἐνεδύσασθε; Acts viii. 16: εἰς τὸ ὄνομα τοῦ κυρίου Ἰυ. The other connections also—ἐπὶ τῷ ὀνόματι Ἰυ, Acts ii. 38; ἐν τῷ ὀν· τοῦ κυρίου, Acts x. 48—in which the word occurs, are favorable to this explanation, so far as they show that what the word was designed to indicate was; so far as εἰς was used, the *relation* into which the baptized were placed; so far as ἐπὶ and ἐν were used, the basis or ground on which baptism was administered. The βαπτίζεσθαι ὑπὲρ τῶν μεκρῶν in 1 Cor. xv. 29 is a baptism on account of the dead; ὑπέρ assigns the motive, as often in Prof. and N. T. Greek; cf. Rom. xv. 8. Plat. Conviv. 208, D: ὑπὲρ ἀρετῆς ἀθανάτου καὶ τοιαύτης δόξης εὐκλεοῦς πάντες πάντα ποιοῦσιν. It is not said that the baptism was for the advantage of the dead, but that the dead—so far, namely, as they will rise again—give the living occasion to be baptized; cf. Acts xvii. 32; that those who have undergone baptism for such a reason have no hope (τί ποιήσουσιν), and have therefore been

baptized in vain (τί καὶ βαπτίζονται) if the dead do not rise at all. Βαπτίζεσθαι ὑπὲρ τῶν νεκρῶν is parallel, therefore, with τί καὶ ἡμεῖς κινδυνεύομεν (v. 30), εἰ νεκροὶ οὐκ ἐγείρονται, vs. 29, 32.

Metaphorical use of βαπτίζειν in Matt. iii. 11: βαπτ. ἐν πνεύματι ἁγίῳ καὶ πυρί opp. ἐν ὕδατι εἰς μετάνοιαν; cf. Luke iii. 16; John i. 33. That the meaning "wash unto purification from sin" is metaphorical, and not that of "immerse," is clear from the contraposition of ἐν ὑδ. and ἐν πν., by which the two baptisms are distinguished from each other. Both in the case of John and of the Messiah the question was one of washing for purification from sin, which the former effected by means of water, the latter by means of the Holy Spirit and fire; cf. Ezra xxxvi. 25-27; Mal. iii. 2, 3; Isa. vi. 6, 7. (It makes no material difference whether ἐν be taken locally or instrumentally: in the one case βαπτίζειν retains firmly the idea of an immersion; in the other case, of a washing, a streaming over.) No distinction is drawn between the baptism which Christ adopted from John and transmitted to his disciples and John's own baptism; it is only said what Messiah's work is in relation to John's; cf. Acts i. 5. It follows, however (coll. Acts ii. 38) that the baptism enjoined by Christ, not pointing to something future, but to something present (Acts xix. 4, 5), must have conjoined with the use of water, the element of which John had opened up the prospect; in other words, that it was a baptism ἐν ὕδατι καὶ πνεύματι or πυρί; cf. John iii. 5.

The use of the word in Luke xii. 50—βάπτισμα δὲ ἔχω βαπτισθῆναι; Mark x. 38, 39: τὸ βάπτισμα ὃ ἐγὼ βαπτίζομαι βαπτισθήσεσθε—was probably suggested by O. T. expressions like Ps. lxix. 2, 3, 15, 16; xlii. 7; cxxiv. 4, 5; clxiv. 7; Isa. xliii. 2; cf. Apoc. xii. 15, not by its employment in the sense to baptize for purification from sin, in opposition to Mark x. 39, as Theophyl. on Matt. xx. 22—βάπτισμα ὀνομάζει τὸν θάνατον αὐτοῦ, ὡς καθαρτικὸν ὄντα πάντων ἡμῶν—assumes. The active and passive occur in Matt. iii. 11, 13, 14, 16; xxviii. 19; Mark i. 4, 8; vi. 14; x. 38, 39; xvi. 16; Luke iii. 16; John i. 25, 26, 28, 31, 33; iii. 22, 23, 26; iv. 1, 2; x. 40; Acts i. 5; viii. 16, 36, 38; x. 47, 48; xi. 16; xix. 3, 4; Rom. vi. 3; 1 Cor. i. 13-17; xii. 13; Gal. iii. 27. The middle = *let one's self be baptized;* with the aor. 1 both pass. and mid. (cf. Krüger, § 52, 6, 1, 4; cf. Matt. iii. 13, 14; Mark x. 38, 39; xvi. 16; Luke xi. 38, for the notion that in this case the middle is properly a mid. passive, and that the verbs in question, owing to the affinity between this meaning and that of the passive, hover between the pass. and mid. aor.; Acts xxii. 16; 1 Cor. x. 2), Matt. iii. 6; Mark i. 5, 9; Luke iii. 7, 12, 21; vii. 29, 30; xii. 50; John iii. 23; Acts ii. 38, 41; viii. 12, 13; xvi. 15, 33; xviii. 8; xxii. 16; 1 Cor. x. 2 (where L. reads ἐβαπτίσθησαν instead of ἐβαπτίσαντο, the mid. to be explained with a regard to Ex. xiv. 31); 1 Cor. xv. 29. Cremer's *Biblico-Theological Lexicon of N. T. Greek*, Edinburgh, 1872.

[7] See Cunningham's *Dissertation on the Epistles of St. Barnabas*, Hulsean Lectures for 1874.

[8] "Ὅτι ἡμεῖς μὲν καταβαίνομεν εἰς τὸ ὕδωρ γέμοντες ἁμαρτιῶν καὶ ῥύπον, καὶ ἀναβαίνομεν καρποφοροῦντες ἐν τῇ καρδίᾳ τὸν φόβον, καὶ τὴν ἐλπίδα εἰς τὸν Ἰησοῦν ἔχοντες ἐν τῷ πνεύματι."

[9] "Ἔπειτα ἄγονται ὑφ' ἡμῶν ἔνθα ὕδωρ ἐστὶ, καὶ τρόπον ἀναγεννήσεως ὃν καὶ ἡμεῖς αὐτοὶ ἀνεγεννήθημεν, ἀναγεννῶνται. Ἐπ' ὀνόματος γὰρ τοῦ Πατρὸς τῶν ὅλων καὶ Δεσπότε Θεοῦ, καὶ τοῦ Σωτῆρος ἡμῶν Ἰησοῦ Χριστοῦ, καὶ Πνεύματος Ἁγίου τὸ ἐν τῷ ὕδατι τότε λουτρὸν ποιοῦνται."

[10] "Descenderunt igitur in aquam cum illis et iterum ascenderunt. Sed hi vivi descenderunt; at illi qui fuerunt ante defuncti mortui quidem descenderunt, sed vivi ascenderunt."

[11] "καὶ εβαπτίσατο φησὶν ἐν τῷ Ἰορδάνῃ ἑπτάκις. Οὐ μάτην πάλαι Ναιμὰν λεπρὸς ὢν βαπτισθεὶς ἐκαθαίρετο, ἀλλ' εἰς ἔνδειξιν ἡμετέραν· οὐ λεπροὶ ὄντες ἐν ταῖς ἁμαρτίαις διὰ τοῦ ἁγίου ὕδατος, κ.τ.λ."

[12] "Lex enim tinguendi imposita est, et forma præscripta. Ite, inquit, docete nationes, tinguentes eas in nomine Patris et Filii et Spiritus Sancti (Matt. xxviii. 19). Huic legi collata definitio illa: nisi quis renatus fuerit ex aqua et Spiritu, non intrabit in regnum cœlorum (John iii. 5), obstrinxit fidem ad Baptismi. Itaque omnes exinde credentes tinguebantur. Tunc et Paulus ubi credidit, tinctus est (Acts ix. 6). Et hoc est quod Dominus in illa plaga orbationis præceperat: exsurge, dicens, et introi Damascum (ibidem), illic tibi demonstrabitur quid debeas agere, scilicet tingui, quod solum ei dereat."

[13] "Quoniam tanta simplicitate, sine pompa, sine apparatu novo aliquo, denique sine sumptu homo in aqua demissus, et inter pauca verba tinctus."

[14] "Et novissime mandans ut tinguerunt in Patrem et Filium et Spiritum Sanctum, non in unum. Nam nec semel, sed ter, ad singula nomina in personas singulas tinguimur."

[15] "Denique, ut a baptismate ingrediar, aquam adituri, ibi,

sed et aliquanto prius in ecclesia sub antistitis manu contestamur nos renuntiare diabolo, et pompæ, et angelis ejus: dehinc ter mergitamur amplius aliquid respondentes, quam Dominus in Evangelio determinavit."

[16] "Nulla distinctio est, mari quis an stagno, flumine an fonte, lacu an alveo, diluatur, nec quidquam refert inter eos quos Joannes in Jordane, et quos Petrus in Tiberi tinxit."

[17] "Εἶδες, ἀγαπητέ πῶς προεῖπεν ὁ προφήτης τὸ τοῦ βαπτίσματος καθάρσιον. Ὁ γὰρ καταβαίνων μετὰ πίστεως εἰς τὸ τῆς αναγεννήσεως λουτρὸν διατάσσεται τῷ πονηρῷ, συντάσσεται δὲ τῷ Χριστῷ· ἀπαρνεῖται τὸν ἐχθρόν, ὁμολογεῖ δὲ τὸ θεὸν εἶναι τὸν Χριστόν· ἀποδύεται τὴν δουλείαν, ἐνδύεται δὲ τὴν υἱοθεσίαν, ἀνέρχεται ἀπὸ τοῦ βαπτίσματος λαμπρος ὡς ὁ ἥλιος, ἀπαστράπτων τὰς τῆς δικαιοσύνης ἀκτῖνας· τὸ δὲ μέγιστον, ἄνεισιν υἱὸς θεοῦ καὶ συγκληρονόμος Χριστοῦ."

[18] "Οὕτως καὶ τὸ διὰ τοῦ ὕδατος λουτρὸν, σύμβολον τυγχάνον καθαρίου ψυχῆς πάντα ῥύπον ἀπὸ κακίας ἀποπλυνομένης."

[19] "Dominus post resurrectionem mittens apostolos mandat et dixit: Data est mihi omnis potestas in cœlo et in terra. Ite ergo et docete gentes omnes, tingentes eos in nomine Patris et Filii et Spiritus Sancti, docentes eos observare omnia quæcunque præcepi vobis."

[20] "Nam si non mentitur apostolus dicens, quotquot in Christo tincti estis, Christum induistis; utique qui illic in Christo baptizatus est, induit Christum."

[21] "In sacramentis salutaribus, necessitate cogente et Deo indulgentiam suam largiente, totum credentibus conferunt divina compendia. Nec quemquam morere debet quod aspergi vel perfundi videntur ægri cum gratiam dominicam consequuntur, quando Scriptura Sancta per Ezechielem prophetam loquatur, et dicat. . . . Unde apparet, aspersionem quoque aquæ instar salutaris lavacri obtinere; et quando hæc in ecclesia fiunt, ubi sit et accipientis et dantis fides integra, stare omnino et consummari ac perfici posse majestate Domini et fidei veritate."

[22] "Descendit quidem is qui baptizatur peccatis obnoxius et servititutis corruptione detentus; ascendit autem ab ea servitute et peccatis liber, factus filius Dei, et hæres, gratia ipsius factus, cohæres autem Christi, indutus ipsum Christum sicut scriptum est; 'quicunque in Christum baptizati estis Christum induistis.'"

23 " Referring to this testimony of Justin Martyr, Prof. M. Stuart, in the *Bib. Repos.*, 1833, p. 356, says: 'I am persuaded that this passage, as a whole, most naturally refers to immersion; for why, on any other ground, should the convert who is to be initiated go out to the place where there is water? There would be no need of this if mere sprinkling or partial affusion only was customary in the time of Justin.' "

24 " 'Εν τούτοις εβαπτίσθης τοις αγαθοίς νεοφώτιστε, αρραβών σοι γέγονεν αναστάσεως, νεοφωτίστε, ή της χάριτος μύησις· ενέχυρον της εν ουρανώ διαίτης έχεις το βάπτισμα· εμιμήσο τη καταδύσει του δεσπότου τον τάφον· αλλά ανέδυς πάλιν εκείθεν, τα της αναστάσεως έργα προ των έργων θεώμενος."

25 " Το γαρ καταδύσαι το παιδίον εν τη κολυμβήθρα τρίτον και αναδύσαι, τούτο δηλοί τον θάνατον και την τριήμερον ανάστασιν του Χριστού."

26 " Μετά ταύτα, επί την αγίαν του θείου βαπτίσματος εχειραγωγείσθε κολυμβήθραν, ως ό Χριστός από του σταυρού επί το προκείμενον μνήμα. Και ηρωτάτο έκαστος ει πιστεύει εις το όνομα του πατρός, και του υιού, και του αγίου Πνεύματος· και υπωλογήσατε την σωτήριον ομολογίαν, και κατεδύετε τρίτον εις το ύδωρ, και πάλιν ανεδύετε· και ενταύθα, δια συμβόλου την τριήμερον του Χριστού αινιττόμενοι ταφήν," κ.τ.λ.

27 " Λέγει γαρ ό Κύριος· 'Υμείς βαπτισθήσεσθε εν πνεύματι αγίω ού μετά πολλάς ταύτας ημέρας· ού μερική ή χάρις, αλλά αυτοτελής ή δύναμις· ώσπερ γαρ ό ενδύνων εν τοις ύδασι και βαπτιζόμενος, πανταχόθεν υπό των υδάτων περιβάλληται· ούτω και υπό του πνεύματος εβαπτίσθησαν ολοτελώς."

28 " An descendentem in aquam ... liceat iterum interrogare in eadem fide et in aqua iterum intingi ?"

29 " 'Εν τρισίν ουν καταδύσεσι, και ισαρίθμοις ταις επικλήσεσι, το μέγα μυστήριον του βαπτίσματος τελειούται, ίνα και ό του θανάτου τύπος εξεικονισθή, και τη παραδόσει της θεογνωσίας τας ψυχάς φωτισθώσιν οι βαπτιζόμενοι."

30 " Περί δε της εν τω βαπτίσματι ανανεύσεως ουκ οίδα τι επήλθέ σοι ερωτήσαι, είπερ εδέξω την κατάδυσιν τον τύπον των τριών ημερών εκπληρούν. Βαπτισθήναι γαρ τρισάκις μη αναδύντα τοσαυτάκις."

31 " Συνταφώμεν ουν Χριστώ δια του βαπτίσματος, ίνα και συναναστώμεν· συγκατέλθωμεν, ίνα και συνυψωθώμεν· συνανέλθωμεν, ίνα και συνδοξασθώμεν."

32 " Ημείς δε το βάπτισμα παραλαμβάνοντες, εις μίμησιν του Κυρίου και διδασκάλου και καθηγεμόνος ημών, εις γην μεν ού θαπτόμεθα . . .

ἐπὶ δὲ τὸ συγγενὲς τῆς γῆς στοιχεῖον, τὸ ὕδωρ, ἐρχόμενοι, ἐκείνῳ ἑαυτοὺς ἐγκρύπτομεν, ὡς ὁ Σωτὴρ τῇ γῇ καὶ τρίτον τοῦτο ποιήσαντες, τὴν τριήμερον ἑαυτοὺς τῆσ ἀναστάσεως χάριν ἐξεικονίζομεν."

[33] "Et ter mergimur, ut Trinitatis unum appareat sacramentum. . . . Potest unum baptisma et ita dici, quod licet ter baptizemur, propter mysterium Trinitatis: tamen unum baptisma reputetur."

[34] "Præceptis Dei lavandi sumus, et cum parati ad indumentum Christi, tunicas pellicas deposuerimus, tunc induemur veste linea, nihil in sese mortis habente, sed tota candida: ut de baptismo consurgentes, cingamus lumbos in veritate, et tota pristinorum turpitudo celetur."

[35] "Interrogatus es, 'credis in Deum, Patrem Omnipotentem?' Dixisti, 'credo' et mersisti, hoc est, sepultus es. Iterum interrogatus es, 'Credis in Dominum nostrum Jesum Christum?' Dixisti, 'credo' et mersisti. Ideo et Christo es consepultus. Qui enim Christo consepelitur, cum Christo resurgit. Tertio interrogatus es, 'Credis et in Spiritum Sanctum?' Dixisti, 'credo.' Tertio mersisti, ut multiplicem lapsum superioris ætatis absolveret trina confessio."

[36] "Clamat ergo Apostolus, sicut audistis in lectione præsenti: Quoniam quicunque baptizatur, in morte Jesu baptizatur. Quid est in morte? Ut quomodo Christus mortuus est, sic et tu mortem degustes, quomodo Christus mortuus est peccato, Deo vivit et tu superioribus illecebris peccatorum mortuus sis per baptismatis sacramentum, et surrexeris per gratiam Christi. Mors ergo est, sed non in mortis corporalis veritate, sed in similitudine; cum enim mergis, mortis suscipis et sepulturæ similitudinem."

[37] "Hesterno die de fonte disputavemus, cujus species veluti quædam sepulchri forma est; in quem, credentes in Patrem et Filium et Spiritum Sanctum, recipimur et demergimur et surgimus, hoc est, resuscitamur."

[38] "Audi ergo, nam ut in hoc quoque sæculo nexus diaboli solveretur, inventum est quomodo homo vivus moreretur, et vivus resurgeret. Quid est vivus? Hoc est vita corporis vivens, cum veniret at fontem et mergeretur in fontem. Quid est aqua, nisi de terra? Satisfit ergo sententiæ cœlesti sine mortis stupore. Quod mergis, solvitur sententia illa: terra es, et in terram ibis; impletâ sententiâ, locus est beneficio remedioque cœlesti. Ergo aqua de terra possibilitas autem vitæ nostræ non admittebat ut terra operiremur, et de terra

resurgeremus. Deinde non terra lavat, sed aqua lavat ; ideo fons quasi sepultura est."

³⁹ " Θεῖα τελεῖται ἐν αὐτῷ σύμβολα· τάφος καὶ νέκρωσις, καὶ ἀνάστασις καὶ ζωὴ, καὶ ταῦτα ὁμοῦ γίνεται πάντα. Καθάπερ γὰρ ἐν τινι τάφῳ, τῷ ὕδατι καταδυόντων ἡμῶν τὰς κεφαλὰς, ὁ παλαιὸς ἄνθρωπος θάπτεται, καὶ, καταδὺς κάτω, κρύπτεται ὅλος καθάπαξ· εἶτα ἀνανευόντων ἡμῶν, ὁ καινὸς ἄνεισι πάλιν. Ὥσπερ γὰρ εὔκολον ἡμῖν βαπτίσασθαι καὶ ἀνανεῦσαι, οὕτως εὔκολον τῷ θεῷ θάψαι τὸν ἄνθρωπον τὸν παλαιὸν, καὶ ἀναδεῖξαι τὸν νέον. Τρίτον δὲ τοῦτο γίνεται, ἵνα μάθῃς, ὅτι δύναμις πατρὸς καὶ υἱοῦ καὶ πνεύματος ἁγίου ἅπαντα ταῦτα πληροῖ."

⁴⁰ " Καθάπερ γὰρ τὸ σῶμα αὐτοῦ ταφὲν ἐν τῇ γῇ καρπὸν τῆς οἰκουμένης τὴν σωτηρίαν ἤνεγκεν· οὕτω καὶ τὸ ἡμέτερον ταφέν ἐν τῷ βαπτίσματι, καρπὸν ἤνεγκε τὴν δικαιοσύνην, τὸν ἁγιασμὸν, τὴν υἱοθεσίαν, τὰ μυρία ἀγαθά· οἴσει δὲ καὶ τὸ τῆς ἀναστάσεως ὕστερον δῶρον. Ἐπεὶ οὖν ἡμεῖς μὲν ἐν ὕδατι, αὐτὸς δὲ ἐν γῇ, καὶ ἡμεῖς μὲν κατὰ τὸν τῆς ἁμαρτίας λόγον, ἐκεῖνος δὲ κατὰ τὸν τοῦ σώματος ἐτάφη, διὰ τοῦτο οὐκ εἶπε Σύμφυτοι τῷ θανάτῳ, ἀλλὰ τῷ ὁμοιώματι τοῦ θανάτου."

⁴¹ " Τὸ γὰρ βαπτίζεσθαί καὶ καταδύεσθαι, εἶτα ἀνανεύειν, τῆς εἰς ᾅδου καταβάσεώς ἐστι σύμβολον καὶ τῆς ἐκεῖθεν ἀνόδου. διὸ τὸν τάφον τὸ βάπτισμα ὁ Παῦλος καλεῖ λέγων, Συνετάφημεν οὖν αὐτῷ διὰ τοῦ βαπτίσματος εἰς τὸν θάνατον."

⁴² " Ἐν τρισὶ καταδύσεσι τοῦ σώματος ἓν βάπτισμα τοῖς ἑαυτοῦ μαθηταῖς παρέδωκε," κ.τ.λ.

⁴³ " In hoc ergo fonte, antequam vos toto corpore tingueremus, interrogavimus: Credis in Deum Patrem Omnipotentem? . . . Postquam vos credere promisistis, tertiô capita vostra in sacro fonte demersimus. Recte enim tertio mersi estis, qui accepistis baptismum in nomine sanctæ Trinitatis. Recte tertio mersi estis, qui accepistis baptismum in nomine Jesu Christi, qui die tertia resurrexit a mortuis. Illa enim tertio repetita demersio typum dominicæ exprimit sepulturæ, per quam Christo consepulti estis in baptismo, et cum Christo resurrexistis in fide: ut peccatis abluti in sanctitate virtutum Christum imitando vivatis."

⁴⁴ " Αὐτὸς καὶ τοῦ ἁγίου βαπτίσματος ἀνέτρεψε τὸν ἀνέκαθεν παρὰ τοῦ κυρίου καὶ ἀποστόλων παραδοθέντα θεσμὸν, καὶ ἀντικρυς ἀντενομοθέτησε, μὴ χρῆναι λέγων τρὶς καταδύειν τὸν βαπτιζόμενον, μηδὲ ποιεῖσθαι τὴν τῆς Τριάδος ἐπίκλησιν· ἀλλ' ἅπαξ βαπτίζειν εἰς τὸν θάνατον τοῦ Χριστοῦ."

⁴⁵ " Φασὶ δέ τινες, πρῶτον τοῦτον Εὐνόμιον τολμῆσαι εἰσηγήσθαι

ἐν μιᾷ καταδύσει χρῆναι επιτελεῖν τὴν θείαν βάπτισιν, καὶ παραχαράξαι τὴν ἀπο τῶν αποστόλων εἰσέτι νυν ἐν πᾶσι φυλαττομένην παράδοσιν."

[46] "Sepulturam triduanam imitatur trina demersio, et ab aquis elevatio resurgentis instar est de sepulchro."

[47] "Baptismum igitur Christi nobis est sepultura in quo peccatis moriemur, criminibus sepelimur, et veteris hominis conscientia resoluta, in alteram nativitatem rediviva infantia reparamur. Baptismum, inquam, Salvatoris nobis est sepultura, quia et ibi perdidimus antè quod viximus, et ibi denuo accipimus, ut vivamus. Magna igitur sepulturæ hujus est gratia, in qua nobis et utilis mors infertur, et vita utilior condonatur; magna, inquam, hujus gratia sepulturæ, quæ et purificat peccatorum et vivificat morientem."

[48] "Hic in fonte homo mergitur."

[49] "In hoc ergo fonte antequam vos toto corpore tingeremus, interrogavimus: credis in Deum Patrem Omnipotentem?" etc.

[50] "Adeo corpus Christi Domini in terra sepultum, sic et nostrum corpus per baptisma sepultum. Nam tres obitus et ortus, hoc est, triplex illa tinctura, mortem et resurrectionem significant."

[51] "Neque enim credendum est eos fuisse baptizatos, qui non in nomine Patris et Filii et Spiritus Sancti juxta regulam a Domino positam tincti sunt."

[52] "Ille post confessionem vel aspergitur aqua, vel intingetur, martyr vero vel aspergitur sanguine, vel contingatur igne."

[53] "Deinde per singulas vices mergis eum tertio in aqua. Postea cum ascendit a fonte," etc.

[54] "Nuntiantur hæc antistiti, qui gaudio magno repletus, jussit lavacrum præparari. Velis depictis adumbrantur plateæ, ecclesiæ cortinis albentibus adornantur, baptisterium componitur, balsama diffunduntur, micant flagrantes odore cerei, totumque templum baptisterii divino respergitur ab odore; talemque ibi gratiam adstantibus Deus tribuit, ut æstimarent se paradisi odoribus conlocari. Rex ergo prior poposcit se à pontifice baptizari. Procedit novus Constantinus ad lavacrum, deleturus lepræ veteris morbum, sordentesque maculas gestorum antiquorum recenti latice deleturus. Cui ingresso ad baptismum, sanctus Dei sic infit ore facundo:

Mitis depone colla, Sicamber, adora quod incendisti, incende quod adorasti.' Igitur rex Omnipotentem Deum in Trinitate confessus, baptizatus est in nomine Patris, et Filii, et Spiritus Sancti, delibutusque sacro chrismate cum signaculo crucis Christi. De exercitu verò ejus baptizati sunt amplius tria millia. Baptizata est et soror ejus Albofleda, quæ non post multum tempus migravit ad Dominum."

[55] " Et ingrediuntur presbyteri aut diaconi, etiam si necesse fuerit, acolythi discalceati, induentes se aliis vestibus mundis, et ingrediuntur ad fontes intro in aqua, et accipientes eos a parentibus suis baptizantur primi masculi, deinde feminæ sub trina mersione, tantum Sanctam Trinitatam semel invocantes, ita dicendo: Baptizo te in nomine Patris, et mergis semel; et Filii, et mergis iterum; et Spiritus Sancti, et mergis tertio."

[56] " Multi sunt, qui in nomine solummodo Christi una etiam mersione se adserunt baptizare. Evangelicum vero præceptum, ipso Deo et Domino salvatore nostro Jesu Christo tradente, nos admonet, in nomine Trinitatis trina etiam mersione sanctum baptisma unicuique tribuere, dicente Domino discipulis suis, 'Ite, baptizate omnes gentes in nomine Patris, Filii, et Spiritus Sancti.' "

[57] " Demerge me Iordanicis fluentis his, quemamodum quæ me genuit infantilibus involvit panis."

[58] " Baptizet sacerdos sub trina mersione, tantum sanctam Trinitatem semel invocans, ita dicendo: Baptizo te in nomine Patris, et mergat semel, et Filii, et mergat iterum, et Spiritus Sancti, et mergat tertiô."

[59] " De trina mersione baptismatis, nil responderi verius potest, quam quod ipsi sensistis: quod in una fide nihil afficit sanctæ ecclesiæ consuetudo diversa. Nos autem quod tertio demergimus, triduanæ sepulturæ sacramenta signamus, ut dum tertio infans ab aquis educitur, resurrectio triduani temporis exprimatur. Quod si quis forte etiam pro summæ Trinitatis veneratione æstimet fieri, neque ad hoc aliquid obsistit, baptizando semel in aquis mergere, quia dum in tribus personis una substantia est, reprehensibile esse nullatenus potest, infantem in baptismate in aquam vel ter vel semel immergere, quando et in tribus immersionibus personarum Trinitas, et in una potest divinitatis singularitas, designari. Sed quia nunc hucusque ab hæreticis infans in baptismate tertio mergebatur, fiendum apud vos esse non censeo: ne dum mersiones enumerant, divinitatem dividant."

[60] "Baptizabit in fluvio Swalua, qui vicum Cataractam præter fluit. Nondum enim oratoria vel baptisteria in ipso exordio nascentis ibi ecclesiæ poterant ædificari."

[61] "Non oportere ter mergere eum qui baptizetur." Can. VI. In Can. V. we find:

"Propter vitandum schismatis scandalum, vel hæretici dogmatis usum, simplam teneamus baptismi mersionem, ne videantur apud nos, qui tertio mergunt, hereticorum probare adsertionem, dum sequuntur et morem. Et ne forte cuique sit dubium hujus simpli mysterium sacramenti, videat in eo mortem et resurrectionem Christi significari: nam in aquis mersio, quasi in infernum descensio est, et rursis ab aquis emersio, resurrectio est. Item videat in eo unitatem, dum semel immergimus; Trinitatem, dum nomine Patris, et Filii, et Spiritus Sancti baptizamus."

[62] "Un giovanetto, tutto ignudo, è immerso interamente in un nembo di acqua."

[63] "Numquid Christus Dominus adspersione baptizatus? Tantum abest a vero, ut nihil magis vero possit esse contrarium, sed errori et inscientiæ pictorum tribuendum, qui quum historiarum sæpe sunt ignari, vel quia quidlibet audendi potestatem sibi factam credunt, res, quas effigunt, mirifice aliquando depravant."

[64] "Nam videtur quidem baptizandus in fontem descendere, videtur aquis intingi, videtur de aquis ascendere; quod autem in illo lavacrum regenerationis egerit, minime potest videri. Sola hoc fidelium novit pietas, quia peccator in fontem descendit, sed purificatus ascendit; filius mortis descendit, sed filius resurrectionis ascendit; filius prævaricationis descendit, sed filius reconciliationis ascendit; filius iræ descendit, sed filius misericordiæ ascendit; filius diaboli descendit, sed filius Dei ascendit."

[65] "Βεβαπτίσμεθα δὲ κατὰ τὸν θάνατον αὐτοῦ τοῦ Χριστοῦ, καὶ τὴν ἀνάστασιν αὐτοῦ. Διὰ γὰρ τῆς ἐν τῷ ὕδατι καταδύσεώς τε καὶ ἀναδύσεως, τριπλῆς τε ἐπικλύσεως, τὴν τριήμερον ταθὴν καὶ τὴν ἀνάστασιν αὐτοῦ τοῦ Χριστοῦ ἐξεικονίζομεν καὶ ὁμολογοῦμεν. Ἔτι δὲ καὶ ὅτι αὐτὸς ἐβαπτίσθη ἐν τῷ Ἰορδάνῃ ὑπὸ Ἰωάννου."

[66] "Hoc baptisma, si in nomine S. Trinitatis peractum fuerit, firmiter permanebit, præsertim cum et necessitas exposcit, ut ille, qui in ægritudine detentus est, hoc modo renatus particeps Dei regni efficiatur."

⁶⁷ " Τὸ γὰρ βάπτισμα τὸν τοῦ κυρίου θάνατον δηλοῖ. Συνθαπτόμεθα γοῦν τῷ Κυρίῳ διὰ τοῦ βαπτίσματος, ὡς φησιν ὁ θεῖος Απόστολος."

⁶⁸ " Τύπος τοῦ θανάτου τοῦ Χριστοῦ εστι τὸ βάπτισμα. Διὰ γὰρ τῶν τριῶν καταδύσεων, τὰς τρεῖς ἡμέρας τῆς του κυρίου ταφῆς σημαίνει τὸ βάπτισμα."

⁶⁹ " Ὁ Ἰσραὴλ, εἰ μὴ παρῆλθε τὴν θάλασσαν, οὐκ ἂν ἐχωρίσθη τοῦ φαραώ. Καὶ σὺ ἐὰν μὴ παρέλθῃς διὰ τοῦ ὕδατος, οὐ χωρίσθησῃ τῆς πικρᾶς τυραννίδος τοῦ διαβόλου."

⁷⁰ " In nomine sanctæ Trinitatis trina submersione baptizatur."

⁷¹ " Unam asserentes mersionem fieri debere, triduanamque nostri salvatoris sepulturam in baptismo negligentes, cum apostolus disceret: consepulti enim estis cum Christo in baptismo. (Rom. vi. 4; Col. ii. 12.) Alii vero trinam volentes facere mersionem et in unaquaque mersione invocationem Sanctæ Trinitatis: ac per hoc totas tres personas ter nominare studentes, dum ipsa veritas præciperet. Ite, docete omnes gentes, baptizantes eas in nomine Patris et Filii et Spiritus Sancti (Matt. xxviii. 19). Quid opus est tertio replicare, quod semel dictum sufficit?"

⁷² " Deinde baptizat eum sacerdos sub trina mersione . . . ego te baptizo in nomine Patris, et mergat semel; et Filii, et mergat iterum; et Spiritus Sancti, et mergat tertio."

⁷³ " Ego te baptizo in nomine Patris, et mergit semel; et Filii, et mergit iterum; et Spiritus Sancti, et mergit tertio."

⁷⁴ " Ut baptismus secundum canonica statuta exerceatur, et non alio tempore, nisi pro magno necessitate: et ut omnes generaliter symbolum et orationem Dominicam sciant, et illi qui parvulos de sacro fonte suscipiunt et pro non loquentibus respondent, ob renunciationem Satanæ, et operum et pomparum ejus, seu fidei credulitatem, sciant se fidejussores ipsorum ad Dominum pro ipsa sponsione, ut dum ad perfectionem ætatis pervenerint doceant eos prædictam orationem Dominicam et symbolum; quia nisi fuerint, districte ab eis exigetur, quod pro non loquentibus Deo promittitur. Ideo generaliter omni vulgo præcipimus, hoc memoriæ mandari."

⁷⁵ " Moriemur ergo peccato, quando abrenuntiamus diabolo et omnibus quæ ejus sunt, consepelimur Christo cum sub invocatione Sanctæ Trinitatis sub trina mersione, in fontem lavacri quasi in quodam sepulcrum descendemus; consur-

gimus Christo, cum exuti omnibus peccatis, de fonte quasi sepulchro egredimur."

[76] "Baptismum Græce Latine tinctio interpretatur . . . infans ter mergitur in sacro fonte ut sepulturam triduanam Christi trina demersio mystice designaret, et ab aquis elevatio Christi resurgentis similitudo est de sepulcro."

[77] "Nos autem tertio mergimus . . . infantem in baptismate vel ter vel semel mergere; quando in tribus mersionibus personarum Trinitas, et in una potest divinitatis singularitas designari."

[78] "Sciant etiam presbyteri, quando sacram baptismum ministrant, ut non effundant aquam sanctam super capita infantium, sed semper mergeantur in acria [for aqua]; sicut exemplum præbuit per semet ipsum Dei Filius omni credenti, quando esset ter mergatus in undis Jordanis. Ita necesse est secundum ordinem servari et haberi."

[79] "Baptismum, βάπτισμα Græce, Latine tinctio interpretatur, quæ non tamen ob hoc quod homo in aquam mergitur tinctio dicitur, sed quia Spiritu gratiæ ibi in melius immutetur, et longe aliud quam erat efficitur."

[80] "Potest et hæc trina mersio triduanam Domini sepulturam significare, maxime cum dicat apostolus; quicumque baptizati sumus in Christo Jesu, in morte ipsius."

[81] "Trina submersione baptizatur . . . oportet ergo cum invocatione Sanctæ Trinitatis sub trina mersione baptismum confici."

[82] "Quæ singularis mersio, quamvis tum ita Hispanis complacuit, dicentibus, trinam mersionem ideo vitandam, quia hæretici quidam dissimiles in Trinitate substantias dogmatizare ausi sunt, ad consubstantialitatem Sanctæ Trinitatis negandam: tamen antiquior usus prævaluit et ratio supra dicta. Si enim omnia deserimus, quæ hæretici in suam perversitatem traxerunt, nihil nobis restabit; cum illi in ipso Deo errantes, omnia, quæ ad ejus cultum pertinere visa sunt, suis erroribus quasi propria adplicarint," etc.

[83] This is the conclusion of the paragraph: "Ter baptizandus mergitur in nomine Patris et Filii et Spiritus Sancti, ut Trinitas unum appareat sacramentum; et non baptizatur in nominibus Patris et Filii et Spiritus Sancti, sed in uno nomine, quod intelligitur Deus, juxta apostolorum. Igitur unus Deus, una fides, unum baptisma."

[84] " Dum quidam sacerdotes in quibusdam partibus terræ trinam, quidam simplam mersionem faciunt, a nonnullis schisma esse conspicitur et unitas fidei scindi videtur."

[85] " Trina namque in baptismate immersio triduanam imitatur sepulturam : et ab aquis elevatio, instar est resurgentis de sepulchro."

[86] " Et baptizat sub trina mersione, ita dicendo : ego te baptizo in nomine Patris, et mergit semel, et Filii, et mergit iterum, et Spiritus Sancti, et mergit tertio."

[87] " In morte ergo ipsius baptizati sumus, quoniam sicut ille mortuus est, ita et nos, cum abrenuntiamus diabolo et operibus ejus, sæculo et pompis ejus, quodammodo morimur, dum aquis immergimur. Et quia dixerat mortem ejus nostram significasse mortem, ut ostenderet quia sepultura illius nostram significavit sepulturam, adjecit : consepulti enim sumus cum illo per baptismum in mortem."

[88] " Scimus, et vere scimus, nos prima nativitate te pollutos, secunda nativitate mundatos . . . Commori enim cum Christo, et sepeliri ad hoc tendit, ut cum illo resurgere possimus, et cum illo vivere. . . . Proinde aqua et Spiritus Sancti sociantur causis, sed beneficiis separantur. Requiritur sane in baptismatis sacramentis aqua propter sepulturam, Spiritus Sanctus propter vitam æternam. Sicut ergo Dominus noster Jesus Christus tribus diebus et tribus noctibus corporaliter sub terræ sepulcro conditus fuisse describitur, et homo ita sub cognato terræ elemento trina vice demersus operitur, ac sic vitalis imitatione mysterii dum demergitur sepelitur, dum educitur suscitatur."

[89] " In baptismo, ut enim tribus diebus jacuit Christus in sepulcro, sic in baptismate trina sit immersio."

[90] " Ἐν μὲν γὰρ εἴρηται βάπτισμα, ὥσπερ καὶ πίστις μία, διὰ τὸ ἐπὶ τῇ τελετῇ δηλαδὴ δόγμα, ἐν ὃν ἐν πάσῃ Ἐκκλησίᾳ, τῇ παραλαβούσῃ βαπτίζειν τῇ τῆς τριάδος ἐπικλήσει, καὶ τυποῦν τὸν τοῦ κυρίου θάνατον καὶ τὴν ἀνάστασιν τῇ τρισσῇ καταδύσει καὶ ἀναδύσει."

[91] " Ἡ βαπτισθῆναι λέξις, τὴν δαψίλειαν, καὶ οἱονεὶ τὸν πλοῦτον τῆς μετουσίας τοῦ ἁγίου πνεύματος σημαίνει· ὡς καὶ ἐπὶ τοῦ αἰσθητοῦ ἔχει τι ὁ βαπτιζόμενος ἐν ὕδατι, ὅλον τὸ σῶμα βρήχων, τοῦ λαμβάνοντος ἁπλῶς ὕδωρ οὐ πάντως ὑγραινομένου ἐξ ὅλων τῶν τόπων."

92 " Τουτέστι, τῷ Μωσῇ ἐκοινώνησαν τῆς τε ὑπὸ τὴν νεφέλην σκιᾶς, καὶ τοῦ διόδου τῆς θαλάσσης· ἰδόντες γὰρ αὐτὸν πρῶτον διαβάντα, κατετόλμησαν καὶ αὐτοὶ τῶν ὑδάτων. Ὥσπερ καὶ ἐφ' ἡμῶν, πρῶτον τοῦ Χριστοῦ ἀποθανόντος καὶ ἀναστάντος, βαπτιζόμεθα καὶ αὐτοὶ, μιμούμενοι τὸν θάνατον διὰ τῆς καταδύσεως, καὶ τὴν ἀνάστασιν διὰ τοῦ ἀναδύσεως. Εἰς τὸν Μωσῆν οὖν ἐβαπτίζοντο, ἀντὶ τοῦ, αὐτὸν ἀρχηγὸν ἔσχον τοῦ τύπου τοῦ βαπτίσματος· τυπος γὰρ βαπτισματος ἦν, τό τε ὑπὸ τὴν νεφέλην εἶναι, καὶ τὸ τὴν θάλασσαν διελθεῖν."

93 " Deinde accipiat sacerdos infantem per latera in manibus suis, et interrogato nomine ejus, baptizet eum trina immersione, sanctam Trinitatem invocando, ita dicens, ' N. et ego baptizo te in nomine (et mergat eum semel versa facie ad aquilonem, et capite versus orientem), et Filii (iterum mergat semel versa facie ad meridiem) et Spiritus Sancti.' Amen. (Et mergat tertio recta facie versus aquam.)"

94 " Sub trina immersione sacro fonte intingere."

95 " Recte enim tertio mersi estis. . . . Illa enim trina immersio typum dominæ exprimit sepulturæ."

96 " In baptismate vel ter vel semel mergere, quando tribus mersionibus."

97 " Dum baptizandus aquæ immergitur, mors Christi insinuatur; dum sub aqua latet mersus, sepultura Christi representatur; dum sublematur ex aquis, resurrectio Christi declaratur. Mersio repetitur tertio . . . in baptismo quoque trinam trina mersionem emersio comitatur."

98 " Baptismus dicitur intinctio, id est ablutio corporis exterior."

99 " De immersione vero si quæritur quoties fieri debeat, precise respondemus vel semel, vel ter pro vario ecclesiæ more."

100 " Ut pueri deferrentur ad ecclesiam, et ibi baptizentur in aqua munda trina mersione."

101 " Si quis puerum ter in aqua immerserit in nomine Patris, et Filii, et Spiritus Sancti amen, et non dixerit: Ego baptizo te in nomine P. ——; non est puer baptizatus."

102 " Tunc baptizat eum sub trina immersione, Sanctam Trinitatem semel tantum invocando, sic: Et ego te baptizo in nomine Patris (et immergat semel), et Filii (et immergat secundo), et Spiritus Sancti (et immergat tertio), est habeas vitam æternam."

[103] "Si vero in necessitate puer baptizetur a laico, sequentia immersionem non præcedentia per sacerdotem expleantur."

[104] "Si vero baptizatus fuerit puer a laico, præcedentia et subsequentia mersionem expleantur vel suppleantur a sacerdote."

[105] "Præcipimus, quod in qualibet ecclesia baptismali, sit fons lapideus, decentis amplitudinis et profunditatis; decenter etiam coopertus, in quo parvuli baptizentur . . . et trina semper fiat emersio baptizandi."

[106] "Pueri autem in necessitate baptizati, si forte convaluerint, ad ecclesiam deferantur; ut quæ defuerant, suppleantur: ea scilicet quæ baptismalem immersionem consequi dignoscuntur."

[107] "In immersione expressius repræsentatur figura sepulturæ Christi, et ideo hic modus baptizandi est communior et laudabilior."

[108] "Quamvis tutius est baptizare per modum immersionis (quia hoc habet communior usus) potest tamen fieri baptismus per modum aspersionis, vel etiam per modum effusionis."

[109] "Super fontes autem fiant omnia quæ solent fieri, sola immersione excepta. Si vero dubium fuerit, sub qua forma verborum puer fuerit baptizatus; tunc sacerdos eum baptizet, dum tamen eum immergens dicat: 'Si tu non es baptizatus, ego baptizo te in nomine Patris et Filii et Spiritus Sancti. Amen.'"

[110] "Sacerdos debet puerum tenere per latera, et versa facie ad aquam debet mergere ita, quod habeat caput primo versus orientem, secundo versus aquilonem, tertio versus meridiem."

[111] "Quod in constitutione cavetur de pueris baptizandis, usque ad generale baptismo Paschæ et Pentecostes videlicet reservandis, pro ipsius statuti reverentia quod hactenus videtur esse neglectum, sic duximus declarandum: ut pueri per octo dies ante Pascha, et dies totidem ante Pentecostes nati, si absque periculo servari valeant, usque ad tempora illa reserventur baptizandi; ita tamen quod medio tempore inter nativitatem puerorum hujusmodi et perfectum baptismum recipiant catechismum, solaque diebus baptismi supersit immersio faciendo."

[112] "Statuimus—ut ille, qui baptizat, cum immergit baptizandum in aqua—dicat hæc verba: Petre, ego te baptizo."

[113] "Si timeatur de morte infantis, an æquam nascatur, et caput ejusdem infantis appareat extra uterum, infundat aquam quæ adfuerit, super caput nascentis dicens: Ego te baptizo," etc.

[114] "Vel si vas haberi non possit, fundatur aqua super caput baptizandi. . . . Sed ut infantem ter immergendo in aqua baptizans dicat sic; Petre, vel Martene, ego baptizo te in nomine Patris, et Filii et Spiritus Sancti. Amen. Si tamen una tantum immersio facta fuerint, erat nihilominus baptizatus. . . . Si tamen tanta copia aquæ haberi non possit, ut infans in ea totalitur mergi possit; cum scutella, vel scypho, vel alio vase, aliqua quantitas aquæ super infantem effundatur."

[115] "Ille, que baptizat, quando immergit in aqua baptizandum, dicat hæc verba nihil addendo, subtrahendo vel mutando, puerum nominando Petre vel Johannes: Ego te baptizo in nomine Patris et Filii et Spiritus Sancti. Et ut caveatur periculum baptizandi, non mergatur caput pueri in aqua, sed sacerdos super verticem pueri ter infundat aquam cum pelvi, vel alio mundo vase et honesto, tenens puerum nihilominus una manu discrete."

[116] "Tempore partus aquam habeant promtam, in quam, si oportuerit, baptizandum immergant dicentes: Ego baptizo—. Aqua, in qua puer immersus fuerit, in baptisterium effundatur."

[117] "Statuimus, quod caput ter in aqua ponatur, nisi fuerit debelis vel infirmus, vel frigidum tempus; tunc aqua per manum sacerdotis super caput pueri profundatur, ne propter submersionem vel frigiditatem vel debilitatem puer extinquatur et moriatur."

[118] "Ter in modum crucis immergat illum in aquam calidam vel frigidam."

[119] "Dreyzehn hundert Jahre war das Taufen allgemein und ordentlich ein Untertauchen des Menschen unter das Wasser, und nur in ausserordentlichen Fallen ein Besprengen oder Begiessen mit Wasser; letzteres ward ausser dem als Taufweise bezweifelt, ja sogar verboten."

[120] "Presbyteri . . . studeant providere, ne in collatione ipsius baptismi, tam in prolatione formæ verborum debita, quam immersione in aqua, circa quæ tota virtus baptismi versatur, aliqua negligentia committatur. Forma autem. . . .

immersio vero fiat trina, sic, quod primam faciat statim, cum incipit formam verborum proferre, ultimam autem finiendo formam."

[121] Wall, *History of Infant Baptism*, vol. ii. p. 307, says the connection shows that these words "do not suppose any other way than dipping used ordinarily ; but only in a juncture of necessity, or fear of the infant's death."

[122] "Quoties debet immergi? Secundum consuetudinem ecclesiæ, vel semel propter imitatem divinæ essentiæ, vel ter propter Trinitatem Personarum."

[123] " "Ὅτι μὲν ἀναγκαῖόν ἐστι καὶ τὸ διὰ τριῶν καταδύσεων φανερόν· ὄυτω γὰρ ὑπὸ τῶν ἁγίων παρεδόθη."

[124] John i. 33: "Mer dye my sande to doepen in den waeter." Matt. iii. 11: "Enn verwar ik dope uw in den waeter."

[125] "Et in immersione vel perfusione servetur consuetudo hujusque introducta."

[126] John i. 33: "Aber der mich sandt zu tauffen im wasser." Matt. iii. 11: "Und furwar ich teuff euch im wasser."

[127] "Sacerdos ter mergendo vel ter abluendo infantem cum aqua dicat."

[128] "Baptisa infantem sub hac forma verborum : Et te baptizo in nomine Patris, superfunde in modum crucis primo, et Filii, superfunde," etc.

[129] "Conferatur (baptismus) . . . adeo, quod super baptizando aqua pura et elementalis sub hac forma verborum fundatur: N. ego baptizo."

[130] "Da nehme er das Kind und tauche es in die Taufe."

[131] "Und wiewohl an vielen Orten der Brauch nimmer ist, die Kinder in die Taufe gar zu stossen und zu tauchen, sondern man sie allein mit der Hand aus der Taufe begeusst, so sollt es doch so seyn und wäre recht, dass man nach Laut des Wörtleins das Kind oder Yeglichen, der getauft wird, ganz hinein ins Wasser senkte und taufte und wieder herauszöge. Darum sollte man der Bedeutung genugthun und ein recht vollkommenes Zeichen geben."

[132] "Hac ratione motus, vellem baptizandos penitus in aquam immergi, sicut sonat vocabulum et signat mysterium, non quod necessarium arbitur, sed quod pulcrum foret, rei

tam perfectæ et plenæ signum quoque et perfectum dari, sicut et institutum est sine dubio a Christo."

[133] "Primo nomen baptismus Græcum est; Latine potest verti mersio, cum immergimus aliquid in aquam, ut totum tegatur aqua. Et quamvis ille mos jam aboleverit apud plerosque (neque enim totos demergunt pueros, sed tantum paucula aqua perfundunt) debebant tamen prorsus immergi, et statim retrahi."

[134] "Unter anderen hätte sich zugetragen dass, da sie mit einander geredt und lange gelesen, Hans Brubbach von Zuricken aufgestanden, geweinet und geschryen. Er wäre ein grosser sünder, und sie sollten Gott für ihn bitten. Hierauf hätte ihn Blaurock gefraget, ob er der gnade Gottes begehrte? Jener hätte geantwortet, ja. Da wäre Mantz aufgestanden, und hätte gesagt: Wer will es mir wehren, dass ich diesen nicht taufe? Auf dieses hätte Blaurock geantwortet, Niemand. Darauf hätte er ein Gatze mit wasser genommen, und ihn getauffet in dem Nahmen des Vaters, des Sohns, und des Heiligen Geistes. Nach diesem wäre Hottinger aufgestanden, und hätte der Taufe begehrt. Denselbigen hätte Mantz auch getauffet."—J. C. Füslin's *Beiträgen zur Erläuterung der Kirchen-Reformationsgeschichte des Schweitzlandes*, Theil, I. s. 265 f.

[135] "Dass Mantz und Blaurock zu ihnen gekommen, und nach dem Nachtmahl in dem Testament gelesen. Da seye Hans Brubbach aufgestanden, hätte seine sünden beklaget und beweinet, die er gethan hätte und ein Zeichen seiner Bekehrung begehrt, nemlich dass man ihn in dem Name des Vaters des Sohns und des Heiligen Geistes besprützen solte. Da habe ihn Blaurock besprützet. Hernach, hat er [Bossart] des Zeichens auch begehret. Da hab ihn Blaurock auch besprützet."—*Füslin*, II. s. 361, 2.

[136] "Und habe ein Hand voll Wasser genommen, und ihn getaufft."—J. H. Ottius, *Annales Anabaptistici*, s. 31.

[137] "Es gelüste ihn schier auch einmal zu sehen wie es doch zuging wenn man einander taufte. Aberlin hätte gesagt; man tauffte also. In dem er mit den händen Wasser aus einem Haffen darinnen er Schue geweichet genommen, und auf ihn gesprützt."—*Füslin*, III. s. 239.

[138] Quoted by Dr. Barnas Sears from an old chronicle. He refers also to Schumm's *History of the Parish of Waldshut*.

139 "Wolffgang Uoliman, . . . ist er uff der fart zu Schaffhussen an den Cunradt Grebel gestossen und by im in so hoche erkantnus des widertouffens kommen, das er nitt wolt mitt ainer schussel mitt wasser allain begossen, sunder gantz nackend und bloss, hinuss in dem Rhin von dem Grebel under getruckt und bedeckt werden."

140 "Täuffen im wasser ist den bekennenden seiner sünder auss dem Gölichen bevehl mit eusserlichen wasser übergiessen und den in die zal der sundern auss eygner erkantnüss und bewilligung einschreiben."

141 "Begerstu nun auff disen glauben und pflicht in wasser nach der einsetzung Christi getaufft, eingeleibt, und also in die eusserlichen Christlichen kirchen eingeschriben werden, zu verzeyhung deiner sünden. So sprich, ich beger es auff die krafft Gottes.
"Ich tauff dich in dem namen des Vaters un sons des heiligen geysts, zu verzeyhung deiner sünden. Amen."

142 "Dinen bader- (ich hab missredt) toufgsellen."—Zwingli's *Werke*, Schuler u. Schulthess, Band II. s. 344.

143 "Das wasser angiessend oder tunkend (for tauchend)."—*Werke*, Band II. s. 240.

144 "Wüssend jr nit, dass welcher in das wasser (damit man in in Christum sichtbarlich fürt und pflichtet) getunkt wirt, dass er in den tod Christi getunkt wirt, das ist, in den tod Christi hinyn gestossen? . . . Sehend jr nit, dass, so wir in das wasser gstossen, glych als vil als begraben werdend in Christum, das ist, in sinen tod, dass wir damit bedütend, dass wir ouch der welt gestorben sygind?"—*Werke*, Band II. s. 253.

145 "Weñ man das kind zum wasser bringt, vnd in der begiessüg oder besprengung spricht: Ich tauff, etc."—*Mittheilungen aus dem Antiquariate*, von S. Calvary & Co., Band I. s. 242.

146 "Demnach nimpt der Diener das kind uff sin Hand uber den Tauff, und spricht zu den Gevätteren: Wöllend ihr nun, dass das kind getaufft werde in dem Tauff uns. Herrn J. Christi, so sprächend Ja und nennend das kind. Hie antwortend die Gevätteren Ja, und nennend das kind. Daruff der Diener dem kind drymalen das Wasser augüsst und spricht, Ich töuff dich," u.s.w.

147 "Die Taufe ist nach der Einsetzung des Herrn ein Bad der Wiedergeburt, welches der Herr seiner Auserwählten mit

einem sichtbaren Zeichen durch den Dienst der Kirche, wie oben gesagt und erläutert ist, anbietet und darstellt.

"In diesem heiligen Bade taufen [in the Latin version of the confession, *tingimus*] wir unsre Kinder," u. s. w. art. 21 [22].—See Schaff's *Creeds of Christendom*, vol. iii., p. 224.

[148] "In baptismo quidem trina illa nostri in aqua immersio, rursusque ter facta ex aqua emersio, et cum Christo nos sepeliri in fide veræ Trinitatis, et cum Christo item resurgere in eadem fide denotat."

[149] "Een tweeden noemt oock Paulus de Doope een Waterbadt der Wedergeboorten. . . . Maer een indruckinge in't water."—*Wercken*, Amsterdam, 1681, p. 13.

[150] "Hoe neerstelijk wy ook soeken des nachts ende daegs, soo bevinden wy nochtans niet meer dan een doopsel in den water dat Godt aengenæm is, uytgedruckt ende begrepen in Godts woort, namelijck, dit doopsel op den Geloove. . . . Maer dit andere Doopsel, namelijk der onmondiger kinderen, en vinden wy immers niet."

[151] "Quanquam et ipsum baptizandi verbum mergere significat, et mergendi ritum veteri ecclesiæ observatum fuisse constat."

[152] "So heist jn der teüffer sich mit gebognē knien vor Gott vn seiner kirchen demütigen, vnd nimet ein rein wasser, vnd geüsst es auff jn, vnd spricht. Ich teüffe dich im Namen des Vaters, Sūns, vn des Heiligen Geists."

[153] Quoted by Wall, *History of Infant Baptism*, vol. ii. pp. 305, 306.

[154] "Baptismus est integra actio, videlicet mersio et verborum pronunciatio. . . . Ego baptizo te, id est, ego testificor hac mersione, te ablui a peccatis," etc.

[155] "Alsdann begiesse der Kirchendiener das Kind, auffgewickelt, wit Wasser und spreche mit heller, lauter und deutlicher Stimme, 'N. Ich tauff dich," u.s.w.

[156] "Tum minister, coram quo super mensam opposita est aqua pura puta in pelvi, puellum baptizat, aquam manu capiti injiciens his verbis: Ego, N. baptizo te," etc.

[157] "Alsdann begiesse der Kirchendiener das Kind dreimal mit einer ziemlichen Hand voll Wassers, und spreche mit heller, lauter und deutlicher Stimme, N. Ich tauffe dich," u.s.w.

[158] "Mox minister puerum ter aqua aspergit (non immergit), dicens."

[159] "Darnach soll der Pfarrherr das Kind unaufgebunden nehmen, und Wasser auf den Kopf giessen, mit dem namen nennen und sprechen, N. Ich tauffe dich," u.s.w.

[160] "Il a donc commandé de baptiser tous ceux qui sont siens, au nom du Père et du Fils et du Saint-Esprit, avec eau pure: nous signifiant par cela que comme l'eau lave les ordures du corps quand elle est répandue sur nous, laquelle aussi est vue sur le corps du baptisé, et l'arrose; ainsi le sang de Christ par le Saint-Esprit, fait le même intérieurement en l'âme, l'arrosant et nettoyant de ses péchés et nous régénérant d'enfants de colère en enfants de Dieu. . . . Et toutefois ce baptême ne profite pas seulement quand l'eau est sur nous, et que nous la recevons, mais profite tout le temps de notre vie."

[161] "Alsdann sage der Kirchendiener, dass sie das Kind nennen; und darnach begiesse er es mit Wasser und spreche, N. Ich taufe dich," u.s.w.

[162] "Sacerdos manu dextera de fonte hauriens aquam fundat super puerum tribus vicibus."

[163] "Ideoque baptizamus, id est, abluimur, aut adspergimur aqua visibili."

[164] "Da nehme er das Kind und begiesse es dreimal mit Wasser und spreche; und Ich taufe dich," u.s.w.

[165] "Der Pastor sol bey dem Haupt stehen, vnnd ihn mit dem Kopff dreymal gar unter das wasser tauchen, Zum ersten, mit dem worten: N. Ich taufe dich in dem Namen Gottes des Vatters, Zum andern, und des Sons, Zum dritten, und des heiligen Geistes. Und die Gefattern sollen an beiden seiten stehen, und der Teuffling bey den Armen halten, und als offt ihn der Priester eintauchet, ihn widerumb empor ziehen und heben."

[166] "Consuetudo ecclesiæ est observanda in baptismo, quoad immersionem vel aspersionem, videlicet: quod, ubi est consuetudo, quod puer immergatur in aquam, debet immergi, nisi timor esset de vita ex causa rationabili et evidenti; et ubi est consuetudo, quod aspergatur sive effundatur aqua super caput sine immersione, illa etiam observanda est."

[167] "Alsdann soll die Hebamm oder ein andere Frau das Kindlein auflösen, und der Kirchendiener dasselbige auf die

Hand nehmen und die Gevatterleute bei den Händlein und Kopf angreifen und halten; und soll der Priester mit der andern Hand das Kindlein ausgewickelt dreimal mit Wasser reichlich begiessen, besprengen, und folgende Wort mit sonderm Ernst und Andacht gar fein langsam, laut, mit heller, deutlicher, verständlicher Stimme sagen: N. Ich taufe dich."

[168] " Baptizandi ritus accurate servetur: nec vero ullo modo confundatur; ita scilicet, ut pro ecclesiæ usu, per episcopum probato, vel aquæ infusione, vel immersione baptismus ministretur."

[169] "Ministratur baptismus triplici modo: immersione, infusione aquæ et aspersione; sed immersionis modus cum antiquissimi in s. Dei ecclesiæ instituti ritusque sit, idemque in ecclesia Ambrosiana perpetuo retentus; ab ea mergendi consuetudine recedi non licet, nisi imminens mortis periculum instet; tumque vel aquæ infusione vel aspersione ministrabitur, servata illa stata baptizandi forma."

[170] " Id parochus mergendo servabit, ut ab ea parte fontis baptismalis stet, ubi directo obtutu orientem spectet. In immersione hoc servabit, ut infantis latera manu utraque firmiter excipiens, illius supini occiput ter mergat, primo dicens: In nomine Patris, iterum, et Filii, tertio, et Spiritus Sancti. Qua in immersione animadvertet, ut, dum mergit, infantem ne lædat, at aqua vere illius occiput immersione tangat."

[171] " Parochus infantem supinum a patrino sublatum utraque manu excipit, ita ut dextra capiti ejus proprior sit: tum ter occiput mergit in aqua in crucis formam, et mergendo, si certo scit, illum non esse baptizatum, explicate profert: N. Ego te baptizo in nomine Patris, et Filii et Spiritus Sancti. Amen. Quæ verba proferantur, dum ter mergit, semel, dum ait: N. Ego te baptizo in nomine Patris, iterum, dum ait: et Filii, tertio, dum dicit: et Spiritus Sancti. Amen."

[172] " In eadem Ecclesia adest Baptisterium, et adsunt fontes separati a Baptisterio.

" Ad sacri fontis consecrationem parochi civitatis non conveniunt.

" Officium baptizandi pertinet ad duos sacerdotes qui appellantur *Dogmani;* attamen ipsi non baptizant, sed habent substitutum qui eorum vices supplet.

" Baptizant per immersionem."

[173] "Dicit Presbyter puero, et ego baptizo te in nomine Patris, mergat semel et Filii, mergat secundo; et Spiritus Sancti. Amen. Mergat tertio."

[174] "Observent baptizantes trinam immersionem seu effusionem."

[175] "Da nehme er das Kind und tauche es in die Taufe, oder ... begiesse es mit Wasser."

[176] "Tutius et consultius fuerit, modica aqua baptizandum ter perfundere, quam ipsum in aquam mergere."

[177] "1. Quod *unum* tantum baptisma sit et una ablutio, non quæ sordes corporis tollere solet, sed quæ nos a peccatis abluit.

"2. Per baptismum tanquam lavacrum illud regenerationis et renovationis Spiritus Sancti salvos nos facit Deus et operatur in nobis talem justitiam et purgationem a peccatis, ut, qui in eo fœdere et fiducia usque ad finem perseverat, non pereat, sed habeat vitam æternam.

"3. Omnes, qui in Christum Jesum baptizati sunt, in mortem ejus baptizati sunt, et per baptismum cum ipso in mortem ejus consepulti sunt, et Christum induerunt.

"4. Baptismus est lavacrum illud regenerationis, propterea, quia in eo renascimur denuo et Spiritu adoptionis obsignamur ex gratia (sive gratis)."

[178] "Der Diener nehme das Kind und frage, wie es solle genennet werden. Alsdann begiesse ers dreimal mit Wasser auf sein Hauptlein, und spreche: N. Ich taufe dich," u.s.w.

[179] "Ego te baptizo in nomine Patris, +, et Filii, +, et Spiritus Sancti, +. Amen. Ad singulos cruces fundens baptismi aquam super caput baptizandi."

[180] "Patrino vel matrina vel utroque (si ambo admittantur) infantem tenente, sacerdos vasculo seu urceolo accipit aquam baptismalem, et de ea ter fundit super caput infantis in modum crucis et simul verba proferens semel tantum distincte et attente dicit: N. Ego te baptizo in nomine Patris, +, fundat primo, +, et Filii, fundat secundo, et Spiritus Sancti, +, fundat tertio."

[181] "Ubi est consuetudo baptizandi per immersionem, sacerdos accipit infantem, et, advertens ne lædatur, caute caput ejus immergit, et trina mersione baptizat, et semel tantum dicit: N. ——."

[182] "In ecclesiis autem, ubi baptismus fit per mersionem, sive totius corporis, sive capitis tantum, sacerdos accipiat electum per brachia prope humeros . . . ter illum vel caput ejus mergendo baptizet sub trina mersione, s. Trinitatem semel tantum invocando."

[183] "Da nehme er das Kind und besprenge es dreimal mit Wasser, und spreche, und ich taufe dich," u.s.w.

[184] "Da nehme er das Kind und taufe es mit Wasser, und spreche, und ich taufe dich," u.s.w.

[185] Wall, in his *History of Infant Baptism*, vol. ii. p. 303, says: "One would have thought that the cold countries should have been the first that should have changed the custom from dipping to affusion, because in cold climates the bathing of the body in water may seem much more unnatural and dangerous to the health than in the hot ones. . . . But by history it appears that the cold climates held the custom of dipping as long as any; for England, which is one of the coldest, was one of the latest that admitted the alteration of the ordinary way."

[186] "Dann nehme er das Kindlein in die linke Hand und besprenge es über dem Rücken oder auf dem Haupte dreimal."

[187] "On peut baptiser en deux manières; scavoir par immersion, en plongeant tout le corps de l'enfant dans l'eau, ou par ablution, en versant une petite quantité d'eau sur le tête, etc. Il prend avec une petite burette de l'eau baptismate dans le baptistaire, et en versera trois fois en forme de croix fur la tête de l'enfant."

[188]   "BENEDICTVS XIII. PONT. MAX.
　　　　ORD. PRÆDICATORVM.
　HVMANÆ REGENERATIONIS FONTEM
　　　VETERI RITV INSTAVRAVIT
　　　　ANNO SOL. MDCCXXV.
　　　　　PONT. SVI ANNO. II."

[189] "Districte præcipit sancta synodus, ut nemo posthac alia forma utatur, quam quæ in Rituali probato præscripta est, nec ullæ aliæ cærimoniæ in ejusdem sacramenti administratione usurpentur, præter eas, quæ a majoribus nostris institutæ, nobisque traditæ, in Ecclesia Orientali servantur. Ut nimirum Sacerdos puerum omni veste nudatum accipiat diligenter, et baptizet eum, sub trina immersione totum corpus

tegendo, Sanctissimam Trinitatem semel invocans, ac dicens:
Ego te baptizo in nomine Patris, et semel immergat, et ex
aqua educat, et Filii, et secundo immergat, et educat, et Spiritus Sancti, et tertio immergat, et educat. Diaconus autem ad
singulas immersiones respondeat, Amen. Ubi vero adulti
sunt baptizandi, et maxime femine, pudori, et honestati consulentes, non permittimus, ut isti juxta antiquum morem
vestibus suis nudentur, et in Baptisterium immergantur, ut
supra de pueris dictum est; sed volumus, ut illis caput tantum
denudantibus, sacerdos super eorum caput effundat aquam
semel dicens, Ego te baptizo in nomine Patris, et iterum
dicens, et Filii, et tertio dicens, et Spiritus Sancti. Quo ritu
effundendi scilicet super caput aquam, vel etiam solum caput
in aquam immergendi juxta locorum consuetudinem, sacerdos
uti potest; sed tum maxime illo utatur, quando baptizandus
vita periclitaretur, si in aquam totus immergeretur."

[190] "Nullus alio, quam per trinam infusionem, modo baptizet."

[191] "Alsdann begiesse der Kirchendiener das Kind dreimal
mit Wasser, und spreche mit heller, lauter, deutlicher Stimme:
N. Ich taufe dich," u.s.w.

[192] "Licet baptismus fieri possit aut per infusionem aquæ,
aut immersionem, aut per aspersionem; tamen modus, qui
magis in usu est, scil. affusio, pro hujatis ecclesiæ consuetudine
retineatur, ita, ut trina ablutione et non unica, caput, et non
pectus, baptizandi perfundatur."

[193] "En effet le verb βαπτίζω—immergo—n'a qu'une seule
acception. Il signifie litteralement et perpetuellement *plonger*.
Baptême et immersion sont donc identiques, et dire, *baptême
par aspersion*, c'est comme si l'on disait *immersion par aspersion*, on tout autre contresens de la même nature."

[194] " Βαπτίζει αὐτὸν ὁ ἱερεὺς, ὄρθιον αὐτὸν κατέχων· καὶ βλέποντα κατὰ ἀνατολάς, λέγων: Βαπτίζεται ὁ δοῦλος τοῦ θεοῦ, ὁ
δεῖνα, εἰς τὸ ὄνομα τοῦ Πατρὸς, ἀμήν, καὶ τοῦ Υἱοῦ, ἀμήν, καὶ
τοῦ Ἁγίου Πνεύματος, ἀμήν, νυν καὶ ἀεὶ, καὶ εἰς τοὺς αἰῶνας τῶν
αἰώνων. Ἀμήν. Ἑκάστη προσρήσει, κατάγων αὐτὸν, καὶ ἀνάγων.'

INDEX.

A.

ABELARD, 109.
Aberlin, Henry, 131.
Abyssinian Church, baptism in the, 182.
Ænon, situation of, 23, 24.
Agenda of Mentz, 145.
——, second Würzburg, 149.
——, Austrian, 149, 150.
——, second Bamberg, 154.
——, Magdeburg, 158.
——, Nuremberg, 158.
'Ainum, 23.
Albofleda, 76, 229.
Alcuin, 95.
Alford, 28.
Ambrose, 60, 88, 205.
Ambrosian ritual, 204.
American Dutch Reformed Church, baptism in, 203.
Anabaptists, 130, 133, 143, 165, 213.
Apostolic baptism, 17, 18, 19, 20, 21, 22.
Apostolic Canons, 48, 68, 91, 120.
Apostolical Constitutions, 65.
Aquinas, Thomas, 144, 122, 213.
Arians in Spain practise single immersion, 78, 81, 82, 120.
Armandus Gasto von Rohan, 183.
Armenians, ritual of, 84, 184.
Armenian Church, baptism in, 196, 208.
Arnold, Rev. Dr. A. N., 205.
Assemani, 184.
Assembly, Westminster, 161, 163, 168, 213.
Athanasius, 53.
Atto, Bishop of Vercelli, 103.
Augsburg Bible, 127.
Augusti, Dr. J. C. W., 5.
Augustine, 64, 88.

B.

BADEN ritual, 147.
Bamberg *Instructional*, 185, 204.

Bamberg liturgy, 128.
—— second *Agenda*, 154.
Baptism, apostolic, 17, 18, 19, 20, 21, 22.
——, Armenian order of, 84.
——, clinic, 45, 46, 47, 49, 51, 83, 197.
——, exegetical testimony concerning the act of, 28, 29, 30, 31, 32, 33.
——, historical testimony concerning the act of, 33, 34, 35, 36, 37.
——, infant, 122.
—— introduced by John the Baptist, 9, 10, 11.
—— in the Abyssinian Church, 182.
—— in the American Dutch Reformed Church, 203.
—— in the Armenian Church, 196, 208, 214.
—— in the Baptist churches in England and the United States, 211, 212, 214.
—— in the cathedral at Milan, 34, 204, 205.
—— in a Calvinist Congregational church in England, 186.
—— in the Church of England, 195, 201, 208.
—— in the Coptic Church, 184.
—— in the Freewill-Baptist churches, 211.
—— in the Gospels, 16, 17.
—— in the Greek Church, 194, 196, 199, 205, 206, 207, 214.
—— in the Methodist Episcopal Church, 202, 211, 214.
—— in the Nestorian Church, 194.
—— in the Presbyterian Church, 202, 203, 209.
—— in the Protestant Episcopal Church, 186, 201, 202, 209, 214.
—— in the Roman Catholic Church, 200, 201, 204, 214.
—— in the Russo-Greek Church, 181, 190, 200, 208.
——, John's, 11, 13, 14, 15, 16, 22

247

248 INDEX.

Baptism, lay, 107, 113.
——, Luther's order of, 178.
—— of infants, oldest representation of, 103.
—— of Jesus by John, 15, 16.
—— of proselytes, 9, 10, 11, 12, 13.
——, order of, in the Reformed church in Zurich, 138.
——, place of, 43.
——, place of Saviour's, 24.
——, representations of, in early art, 84, 85, 86, 87, 88.
——, Strasburg order of, 133.
——, Venetian order of, 156.
Baptist Quarterly, 215.
Baptists, confession of New Hampshire, 190.
——, Freegrace, 185.
Baptisteries, 88, 121.
Baptistery of Constantine, 89.
—— of Parma, 121, 153.
—— of Pistoja, 124.
—— of Ravenna, 85, 89.
—— of San Sophia, 88.
—— of Verona, 121.
Baptizein, meaning of, 25, 26, 27, 215-223.
Barber, Edward, 158.
Barnabas, Epistle of, 38, 47.
Basil, 48, 56.
Baxter, Richard, 175, 209.
Bede, the Venerable, 79, 93.
Belgic confession, 148.
Benedictus XIII., 177, 244.
Bengel, 9.
Bernard of Clairvaux, 110.
Bernardo, Bishop, 121.
Besançon, Council of, 150.
Bethabara, 22, 24.
Bethany, 22.
Bible, Augsburg, 127.
——, Lower Saxon, 127.
Bingham, 81.
Blake, Rev. Thomas, 160.
Blaurock, George, 130, 131, 238.
Boldetti, 86.
Bonaventura, 115.
Borromeo, Carlo, 151, 152.
Bossart, Marx, 130, 131, 238.
Bottari, 86.
Bourges, Council of, 154.
Brenner, 5, 83, 122.
Brown, Rev. J. N., 190.
Brubbach, John, 130, 131, 238.
Bucer, 139.
Bugati, 88.
Bugenhagen, 135, 136, 137.
Bullinger, 139, 151.
Bunsen, Baron C. C. J., 5, 36, 52.

C.

CALVACASELLA, 85.
Calvary, S., & Co., 6, 239.
Calvin, John, 142, 166, 213.
Canons, Apostolic, 48, 68, 91, 120.
Capito, 139.
Catacomb of San Ponziano, 86.
Catacomb of St. Calixtus, 85.
Cataracta, village of, 230.
Catechism, Anglican, 156, 171, 172
Cathcart, Rev. Dr. W., 6.
Celichyth, Council of, 99, 122.
Charlemagne, 95, 98.
Chrysostom, 62, 83.
Chrystal, Rev. James, 5, 198.
Church of England, baptism in, 195, 201, 208.
Clark, Rev. J. H., 210.
Clement of Rome, 65.
Clinic baptism, 45, 46, 47, 49, 51, 83, 197.
Clovis, King, 74.
Comber, Dean, 174.
Conant, Rev. Dr. T. J., 5, 25, 48.
Conder, C. R., 23.
Confession, Belgic, 148.
——, first Helvetic, 139.
——, of 1643, London, 160, 168.
——, of 1660, London, 171.
——, of 1689, London, 174.
——, New Hampshire Baptist, 190.
——, of Baptist churches in Bucks, Hertford, Bedford, and Oxford Counties, England, in 1678, 172.
——, of Freewill-Baptist churches, 191, 211.
——, of Moravian Anabaptists, 143.
——, of some Baptist churches in Somerset, England, in 1656, 170.
——, Presbyterian, 202.
——, Saxon, 146.
——, second Helvetic, 149.
——, Westminster, 170.
Congregational Union of England and Wales, Declaration of, 190.
Constantine, 88.
——, baptistery of, 89.
Constitutions, Apostolical, 65.
Conybeare, 31.
Cornelius, Bishop of Rome, 46, 47.
Cote, Dr. W. N., 5, 107, 121, 164.
Council of Besançon, 150.
—— Bourges, 154.
—— Calcuith, 97.
—— Carthage, 55.
—— Cashel, 110.
—— Celichyth, 99, 122.

INDEX.

Council of Clermont, 114.
—— Cologne, 116.
—— Exeter, 118.
—— Florence, 126.
—— Neo-Cæsarea, 83.
—— Nicæa, 47, 50, 51.
—— Nismes, 117, 120.
—— Prague, 124.
—— Ravenna, 119, 123, 124, 213.
—— Toledo, 80, 82, 91, 102, 103, 120, 212, 213.
—— Trent, 141, 146.
—— Tribur, 103.
—— Utrecht, 118.
—— Westminster, 113.
—— Worcester, 113, 114, 120.
—— Worms, 102, 120, 213.
—— Zurich, 133.
Cranage, Dr., 209.
Cranmer, 114.
Creeds, origin of, 50.
Cremer, 27, 219, 223.
Cromwell, Oliver, 161.
Crosby, T., 5.
Crowe, 85.
Cunningham's *Diss. on Ep. St. Bar.*, 223.
Cutting, Rev. Dr. S. S., 6.
Cyprian, 44, 49, 50, 212.

D.

DE WETTE, 30.
Dionysius Exiguus, 68.
Döllinger, 35, 199.
Durant, Guillaume, 118.
Dutch Reformed Church order of baptism, 203.
Dwight, H. G. O., 196, 208.

E.

EDMUND, Constitutions of, 113.
Edwards, Morgan, 140.
Edwin, King, 79.
Eigbright, 121.
Ellicott, Bishop C. J., 32.
Ely, Bishop of, 207.
England, ritual in the Church of, 156, 201.
Erasmus, 128.
Espach ritual, 148.
Eunomians, 69, 81, 212.
Eunomius, 69.
Eusebius, 50.
Ewald's *Jahrb. d. Bib. Wiss.*, 217.
Exeter, Council of, 118.

F.

FABIOLA, 60.
Featley, Dr., 158, 169.
Ffoulkes, 24.
Florence, Council of, 126.
Font, baptismal, 107, 118, 167.
Frankfort liturgy, 147.
Frederic, Elector, 149.
Freewill Baptist Confession, 191, 211.
Fritsche, 31.
Fritz, John, or Frith, 1, 136, 137, 138.
Fulbertus, 101.
Füslin, J. C., *Beitragen*, etc., 238.

G.

GARRUCCI, 85.
Geikie, 11.
Gelasius, 72.
Gemara, Babylonian, 13.
Gennadius, 71, 72.
Germanus, 93.
Gerson, John, 125.
Gilbert, 107.
Goadby, Rev. J. J., 6, 159.
Godet, 10.
Gratus, 55.
Grebel, Conrad, 131, 132, 239.
Greek Church, baptism in, 194, 196, 199, 205, 206, 207.
——, ritual in the, 1, 199.
——, Russo-, 200.
Gregory the Great, 77, 81, 82, 212.
——, Bishop of Nyssa, 59.
——, of Nazianzen, 58, 90.
——, Presbyter of Antioch, 77.
——, the Monk, 126.
——, of Tours, 74.
Grimm, C. L. W., 26, 217.
Guericke, 35.

H.

HACKETT, REV. DR. H. B., 24.
Hamburg church discipline, 137.
Helvetic Confession, first, 139.
——, second, 149.
Henry II. of England, 111.
Hermas, Shepherd of, 39.
Herzog's *Realencycl.*, 219.
Hincmar, 100.
Hippolytus, 43, 49.
Höfling, J. W. F., 5, 122.
Horn, Bishop, 151.
Hovey, Rev. Dr. A., 6.
Howard, Luke, 159.
Howson, 31.

Hubmaier, 131, 132, 133, 134.
Hugo of St. Victor, 108.
Hulsean Lectures, 223.

I.

IMMERSION, single, 69, 79–83, 91, 95, 96, 99, 100, 117, 120, 125, 132, 134, 137, 142, 145, 150–156, 158–162, 164–177, 180, 185, 190, 191, 193, 195, 198, 208, 209, 211, 212.
——, trine, 43, 48, 51, 54, 55, 58–60, 62–64, 67–71, 74, 76–79, 81, 82, 91, 94, 96–105, 107, 109, 110, 111, 113–115, 117–121, 124–126, 128, 139, 145, 148, 153, 154, 156, 157, 178, 182, 183, 185, 186, 188, 191, 192, 194, 196, 197, 200, 205, 206–208, 212.
—— in the Church of England at the present time, 208, 209.
Irenæus, 39, 48.

J.

JAMES OF EDESSA, liturgy of, 91.
Jerome, 48, 59, 87.
John Baptist, 216.
—— of Damascus, 94.
——, Bishop of Regensburg, 128.
Jones, Rev. Hugh, 204.
Justin Martyr, 229.

K.

KESSLER, 6, 132.
Kiepert, 23.
Kiffin, William, 159.
Kurtz, 34, 51.

L.

LANDSBERGER, JOHANNES, 134.
Lanfranc, 104.
Lange, 28.
Lay-baptism, 107, 113.
Leander, Bishop of Seville, 81.
Leidradus, 98, 120.
Leo the Great, 70.
—— Juda, 139
—— of Modena, 13.
Lexicon, Cremer's *Biblico-Theological, of New Testament Greek*, 27, 219.
——, Liddell and Scott's *Greek-English*, 26, 215.
—— *of Greek Usage in the Roman and Byzantine Periods*, by Sophocles, 27, 218.

Lexicon, Wilke's *New Testament Greek*, Grimm's ed., 26, 217.
Leyrer, 219.
Lightfoot, 9, 24, 161.
——, Canon, 32.
Limborch, 31.
Liturgy, Bamberg, 128.
——, Frankfort, 147.
——, Scotch, 158.
——, Würzburg, 128.
——, Zurich, 148.
London, Confession of 1643, 160, 168.
—— of 1660, 171.
—— of 1689, 174.
Luther, 128, 136, 165, 178.
Lyndwood, 125.

M.

MABILLON, 111.
Macarius, 197.
Macknight, 31.
Magdeburg *Agenda*, 158.
Magnus, 45, 49, 212.
——, Archbishop of Sens, 99.
Maimonides, 13.
Malan, Rev. S. C., 208.
Mantz, Felix, 130, 238.
Mark of Ephesus, 126.
Maronite synod, 178.
Martyr, Justin, 38, 47.
Maximus, 170.
Menno, 140, 141
Mennonites, 166, 180.
Mentz, *Agenda* of, 145.
Methodist Episcopal Church, order of baptism in, 202, 211, 214.
Meurer, 136.
Meyer, H. A. W., 10, 28, 29, 30, 33.
Milan, baptism in the cathedral of, 204, 205.
Mishna, 10.
Mosheim, 36.
Müller, John, 131.
Myconius, 139.

N.

NEANDER, 51, 217.
Neo-Cæsarea, Council of, 83.
Nestorian ritual, 194.
Netherlands, Council of, 117.
New Hampshire Baptist Confession, 190.
Nicæa, Council of, 47, 50, 51.
Nismes, Council of, 117, 120.
Novatian, 46.
Nuremberg *Agenda*, 158.

O.

OLEARIUS, 181, 182.
Olshausen, 28, 30.
Order of Baptism, Luther's, 128.
——, Strasburg, 133.
——, Zurich, in Reformed Church of, 138.
——, Venetian, 156.
Ordo Romanus, 96.
Ordo Romanus X., 111.
Origen, 39, 44, 49.
Orleans ritual, 154.
Osgood, Dr. Howard, 132, 141.
Ottius, J. H., *Annal. Anab.*, 238.

P.

PACIAUDUS, 86.
Padua, Council of, 127.
Paine, Prof. L. L., 37.
Pallasonus, Johannes, 121.
Palmer, Sir Roundell, 193.
Palmer, Rev. William, 193, 195.
Parma, baptistery of, 121, 153.
Patriarch of Constantinople, 193, 194, 205.
Paulinus, 79, 95.
Pelagius, Pope, 77.
Peter Lombard, 110.
Picart, Bernard, 180, 181, 182.
Pindar, 217.
Pistoja, baptistery of, 124.
Plumptre, E. H., 28, 29.
Pococke, Richard, 183.
Pomeranian ritual, 149.
Pomeranus, 135.
Pope Adrian I., 97.
—— Alexander III., 111.
—— Benedict, 177.
—— Celestine, 119.
—— Leo I., 103.
—— Leo III., 98.
—— Leo X., 139.
—— Paul III., 139.
—— Paul V., 156.
—— Pelagius, 77.
—— Pius IX., 205.
—— Stephen II., 94, 121.
—— Vitalianus, 91.
Pouring, 45–47, 72, 83, 84, 114, 116, 121–127, 129, 132–135, 137, 138, 142–145, 148, 149, 152, 156–158, 161, 163, 165, 166, 170, 172, 176, 179, 180, 183, 184, 186, 193, 200–204, 208, 209, 212.
Prague, Council of, 124.
Prayer, Book of Common, 144, 146.

Prayer-book, revised under Charles II., 172.
—— of Edward VI., 165.
—— of James I., 155.
Presbyterian Church in the United States, order of baptism in, 202, 203, 209, 214.
—— Confession, 202.
Presbyterian, The, 210.
Presbytery of Lackawanna, 210.
Pressensé, 34.
Pride, Rev. E. W., 6.
Proselyte baptism, 9, 10, 11, 12, 13.
Protestant Episcopal Church in the United States, order of baptism in, 201.
Pullus, 109.

Q.

QUINTILLA of Carthage, 41.

R.

RABANUS MAURUS, 99.
Ravenna, baptistery of, 85, 89.
—— Council of, 119, 123, 124, 213.
Remigius, 74, 76.
Remy, 74.
Reuss, 35.
Rhynsburgers, 180.
Richard, Earl of Warwick, 164.
Riedermann, Peter, 143, 144.
Ritual, Ambrosian, 204.
——, Baden of 1556, 147.
——, English Douay of 1604, 156.
——, Espach of 1560, 148.
——, Lower Saxon of 1585, 154.
——, Nestorian, 194.
—— of the Armenians, 184.
—— of Borromeo, 1576, 152.
—— of Church of England, 201, 208.
—— of Elector Frederick of the Palatinate, of 1563, 149.
—— of Greek Church, 200, 205, 206.
—— of Orleans, 1581, 154.
——, Pomeranian, of 1569, 149.
——, Roman, 157.
    now in use, 200, 204.
    of Paul V., 1614, 157.
——, Strasburg, of 1598, 155.
    of 1742, 183.
——, Ulm, of 1747, 184.
——, Weimar, of 1664, 172.
——, Wurtemburg, 146.
Robinson, *History of Baptism*, 5, 186.
Roman Catholic Church, ritual in, 20.

252 INDEX.

Rouse, John, 164.
Russo-Greek Church, baptism in, 181.

S.

SADOLET, JAMES, 139.
Salem, 23, 24.
Salisbury *Use*, 106.
San Sophia, baptistery of, 88.
Sarum *Manuale ad Usum*, 138.
Savoy Conference, 172.
Saxon Confession, 146.
—— ritual, Lower, 154.
—— visitation articles, 154.
Schaff, Dr. P., 5, 33, 122, 144, 240.
Schneckenburger, 215, 219.
Scotch liturgy, 158.
Scythopolis, 23.
Selden, 174.
Sears, Dr. Barnas, 238.
Shalem, 23.
Sharp, Dr., Archbp. of York, 176.
Shepherd, the, 39.
Sicamber, 75.
Simpson on baptismal fonts, 167.
Smith's *Dict. of Antiquities*, 84, 89.
Sohm's *Hist. Waldshut*, 238.
Sophocles, E. A., 27, 218.
Sozomen, 69.
Sprinkling, 114, 119, 122, 123, 125, 130–132, 135, 136, 143, 146, 147, 149, 150, 152–156, 158, 159, 161–163, 165, 166, 168, 170–172, 174, 176, 186, 187, 193, 202, 203, 205, 207, 209, 211, 212.
Stanley, Dean A. P., 23, 24, 34.
Starck, J. A., 6.
Stephen, Bishop of Salona, 68.
Stephen II., Pope, 121.
Stourdza, Alexander de, 187.
Strabo, Walafrid, 100, 120.
Strasburg ritual, 155, 183.
Stuart, Prof. Moses, 229.
Succoth, 23.
Swale, baptism in, 80, 230.
Syra, Archbishop of, 207.

T.

TAYLOR, BAYARD, 196.
Taylor, Jeremy, 171.
Tertullian, 39, 41, 42, 43, 48, 212.
Thayer, Prof. J. H., 26.
Theodolus, 71.
Theodore, Archbishop of Canterbury, 91.
Theodoret, 69.
Theodulphus, 98.
Theophilus, 48.
Theophylact, 105.

Thiersch, 36.
Tholuck, A., 30.
Thomam, Rudolph, 130.
Thring, Rev. E., 209.
Toledo, Fourth Council of, 80, 82, 91, 102, 103, 120, 212, 213.
Towerson, Dr., 173.
Toy, Dr. C. H., 215.
Trent, Council of, 141.
Tyndale, William, 135, 138.

U.

ULIMANN, WOLFGANG, 131, 132, 239.
Ulm ritual, 184.
Usher, Archbishop, 170.
Utrecht, Council of, 118.

V.

VALIER, JOHN DE, SAINT, 176.
Venema, 36.
Verona, baptistery of, 121.
Victor, Hugo St., 108.

W.

WADDINGTON, 35.
Wall, W., 5, 72, 163, 166, 177, 240, 244.
Waterland, 48.
Watson, Bishop of Lincoln, 147.
Weimar ritual, 172.
Wesley, John, 179.
Westminster Assembly, 161, 163, 168, 213.
—— Confession, 170.
—— General Council, 113.
Whitaker, Dr., 166.
White, Bishop William, 187.
Wicliffe, John, 125.
Wilke's *Lexicon of New Testament Greek*, 26, 217.
William the Conqueror, 104, 106.
Williams, Isaac, 192.
Wilson, Bishop, 33.
Winer, *Realwörterbuch*, 219.
Worcester, Council of, 113, 120.
Worms, Council of. 102, 120, 213.
Wurtemburg ritual, 146.
Würzburg liturgy, 128.
—— second *Agenda*, 149.

Z.

ZURICH letters, 150.
—— liturgy, 148.
—— order of baptism, 138.
Zwingli, 133, 134, 151, 239.

A
Biographical Sketch
of
Henry Sweetser Burrage
(1837-1926)

by
John Franklin Jones

A Biographical Sketch of Henry Sweetser Burrage (1837-1926)

Henry Sweetser Burrage was born January 7, 1837 at Fitchburg, Massachusetts to Jonathan Burrage, and Mary T. Upton. The elder Burrage was a manufacturer of varnish. Burrage was the seventh generation descendent from John Burridge of Norforlkshire (imprisoned under Charles I; migrated to Charleston, Mass [1637]). He was the seventh generation from Major Simon Willard, who founded Concord (*DAB*).

He was schooled at Pierce Academy, Middleton (*DAB*); and received the B.A. (*Schaff*) from Brown University (1861), at which place his poetic ability gained him election to Phi Beta Kappa. He went to Newton Theological Seminary, but left after one year to enlist in 36th Massachusetts Volunteer Infantry and rose to the rank of major (*DAB*).

His war experience included receiving a shoulder wound at Cold Harbor (*DAB*) June 3, 1864 (*Schaff*), being captured at Petersburg, and a brief imprisonment at Libby Prison (*DAB*) Nov. 1, 1864, to Feb. 22, 1865 (*Schaff*).

At the conclusion of the war, he resumed his studies at Newton, from which he graduated (1867). He spent 1868-69 at the University of Halle, living in home of Professor Tholuck (*DAB*).

JOHN FRANKLIN JONES

Burrage's only pastorate was the Baptist Church, Waterville, Maine (1869-73) (*DAB*). He moved to Portland and became editor of *Zion's Advocate*, serving as its editor for thirty-two years. This paper "ranked among the best of the provincial religious journals." Burrage singularly managed the paper courteously; it "did not display the dogmatic and disputative temper which marred much contemporary religious journalism" (*DAB*). Burrage greatly enlarged its reputation/influence and, via that publication, engendered a new enthusiasm for education among the churches of Maine. The paper advocated denomination principles and practices (Armitage, 883-4).

He served as recording secretary of the Maine Baptist Missionary Convention (1875 to 1905) (*Schaff*) and the American Baptist Missionary Union and expressed his foreign mission interests therefrom. Various other positions exhibited his widespread usefulness: trustee of Colby College (1881-1906), Newton Theological Institution (1881-1906), and Brown University (1889-1901); Fellow of Brown from 1901(*DAB*); secretary of the Maine Society of Colonial Wars (1899?-1905 (*Schaff*); recorder of the Maine Commandery, Loyal Legion of Civil War veterans (1889-1912) (*DAB*); secretary of the Maine Society of the Sons of the American Revolution (1891-1905) and president of same (1906?-1907) (*Schaff*); and chaplain of the National Soldiers' Home at Togus (1905-12) (*DAB*).

Burrage possessed an intense vocational interest in history and pursued same until his appointment as Maine's state historian (1907). In that official position, he "greatly stimulated the development of the Maine Historical Society" (*DAB*).

Among his most significant writings are (*Brown University in the Civil War* (1868) (*Schaff*); *The Act of Baptism in the History of the Christian Church* (1879); *History of the Anabaptists of Switzerland* (1882) (*DAB*); *Rosier's Relation of Weymouth's Voyage to the Coast of Maine, 1605* (1887) (*Schaff*); *Baptist Hymn Writers and Their Hymns* (1888);

A Biographical Sketch of Henry Sweetser Burrage

History of the Baptists in New England (1894); *History of the Baptists of Maine* (1904) *(DAB)*; *Gettysburg and Lincoln* (1906) *(Schaff)*; *The Beginnings of Colonial Maine, 1602-1658* (1914); *Maine in the Northeastern Boundary Controversy* (1919); and *Maine Historical Memorials* (1922) *(DAB)*. He has also edited *Early English and French Voyages* (1907) *(Schaff)*.

He married Caroline Champlin in 1873 (she died 1875); he married a second wife; Ernestine Maie Giddings in 1881. Burrage died March 9, 1926 *(DAB)*.

BIBLIOGRAPHY

Armitage, Thomas. *A History of the Baptists; Traced by their Vital Principles and Practices, from the Time of Our Lord and Saviour Jesus Christ to the Year 1886.* With an introduction by J. L. M. Curry. New York: Bryan, Taylor, & Co. 1887.

Dictionary of National Biography. S.v. "Burrage, Henry Sweetser," by William Henry Allison.

http://www.ccel.org/ccel/schaff/encyc02.burrage_henry_sweetser.html?bcb=0. Accessed Tuesday, May 23, 2006.

By John Franklin Jones
Cordova, Tennessee
June 27, 2006

THE BAPTIST STANDARD BEARER, INC.

a non-profit, tax-exempt corporation
committed to the Publication & Preservation
of the Baptist Heritage.

CURRENT TITLES AVAILABLE IN
THE BAPTIST *DISTINCTIVES* SERIES

KIFFIN, WILLIAM   A Sober Discourse of Right to Church-Communion. Wherein is proved by Scripture, the Example of the Primitive Times, and the Practice of All that have Professed the Christian Religion: That no Unbaptized person may be Regularly admitted to the Lord's Supper. (London: George Larkin, 1681).

KINGHORN, JOSEPH   Baptism, A Term of Communion. (Norwich: Bacon, Kinnebrook, and Co., 1816)

KINGHORN, JOSEPH   A Defense of "Baptism, A Term of Communion". In Answer To Robert Hall's Reply. (Norwich: Wilkin and Youngman, 1820).

GILL, JOHN   Gospel Baptism. A Collection of Sermons, Tracts, etc., on Scriptural Authority, the Nature of the New Testament Church and the Ordinance of Baptism by John Gill. (Paris, AR: The Baptist Standard Bearer, Inc., 2006).

CARSON, ALEXANDER	Ecclesiastical Polity of the New Testament. (Dublin: William Carson, 1856).
BOOTH, ABRAHAM	A Defense of the Baptists. A Declaration and Vindication of Three Historically Distinctive Baptist Principles. Compiled and Set Forth in the Republication of Three Books. Revised edition. (Paris, AR: The Baptist Standard Bearer, Inc., 2006).
BOOTH, ABRAHAM	Paedobaptism Examined on the Principles, Concessions, and Reasonings of the Most Learned Paedobaptists. With Replies to the Arguments and Objections of Dr. Williams and Mr. Peter Edwards. 3 volumes. (London: Ebenezer Palmer, 1829).
CARROLL, B. H.	*Ecclesia* - The Church. With an Appendix. (Louisville: Baptist Book Concern, 1903).
CHRISTIAN, JOHN T.	Immersion, The Act of Christian Baptism. (Louisville: Baptist Book Concern, 1891).
FROST, J. M.	Pedobaptism: Is It From Heaven Or Of Men? (Philadelphia: American Baptist Publication Society, 1875).
FULLER, RICHARD	Baptism, and the Terms of Communion; An Argument. (Charleston, SC: Southern Baptist Publication Society, 1854).
GRAVES, J. R.	Tri-Lemma: or, Death By Three Horns. The Presbyterian General Assembly Not Able To Decide This Question: "Is Baptism In The Romish Church Valid?" 1st Edition.

	(Nashville: Southwestern Publishing House, 1861).
MELL, P.H.	Baptism In Its Mode and Subjects. (Charleston, SC: Southern Baptist Publications Society, 1853).
JETER, JEREMIAH B.	Baptist Principles Reset. Consisting of Articles on Distinctive Baptist Principles by Various Authors. With an Appendix. (Richmond: The Religious Herald Co., 1902).
PENDLETON, J.M.	Distinctive Principles of Baptists. (Philadelphia: American Baptist Publication Society, 1882).
THOMAS, JESSE B.	The Church and the Kingdom. A New Testament Study. (Louisville: Baptist Book Concern, 1914).
WALLER, JOHN L.	Open Communion Shown to be Unscriptural & Deleterious. With an introductory essay by Dr. D. R. Campbell and an Appendix. (Louisville: Baptist Book Concern, 1859).

For a complete list of current authors/titles, visit our internet site at:
www.standardbearer.org
or write us at:

he Baptist Standard Bearer, Inc.
NUMBER ONE IRON OAKS DRIVE • PARIS, ARKANSAS 72855
TEL # 479-963-3831   *FAX # 479-963-8083*
EMAIL: Baptist@centurytel.net   *http://www.standardbearer.org*

Thou hast given a standard to them that fear thee; that it may be displayed because of the truth. — Psalm 60:4

www.ingramcontent.com/pod-product-compliance
Lightning Source LLC
Chambersburg PA
CBHW021806220426
43662CB00006B/200